English Springer Spaniels

ENGLISH SPRINGER SPANIELS

AN OWNER'S COMPANION
Jan Wood

The Crowood Press

First published in 1995 by
The Crowood Press Ltd
Ramsbury, Marlborough
Wiltshire SN8 2HR

British Library Cataloguing in Publication Data
A catalogue record for this book is available from the British Library.

ISBN 1 85223 924 7

Dedication
To my husband Rob for his great ability to put things in perspective.

Acknowledgements
A very big thank you for help with this book must go to: Mr Harry Hardwicke, Mr and Mrs Ian Hampton, Ms Frances Nelson – USA, Mrs Alice Berd – USA, Mr and Mrs John Peters – Australia, Rachael Greaves – Australia, Sigrun Wallguist – Sweden, Ellen Getz – Norway, Heidi Fosberg – Norway, Rickie Hughes – Eire, Mr Charles Barrett, Soc. Hom. BHMA, Mr Geoff Thorpe B.Sc., MRCVS, Mrs Pam Wadsworth, Mrs Ann Corbett, Mr Phil Timmings and Mr Walter Harrison

Frontispiece: a favourite picture of the author and Sh.Ch. Ardencote Tapestry taken at the National Gundog Championship Show, where she had gone Best Veteran and been shortlisted for BIS.

Picture Credits
The author wishes to thank all those who kindly permitted their photographs to be reproduced in this book, including: Alverson Photographers, Inc., page 73; Ashbey Photography, pages 153, 163; Gosta Axelsson, page 49; K. Barkleigh-Shute, page 159; Lillemore Boos, page 52; C.M. Cooke, pages 27, 157; David Dalton, pages 2, 146; Gibbs, page 25; Alan Grindle, page 30 (both); Hartley, page 172; Jasinsky, page 6; Carol Ann Johnson, pages 125, 129, 132; J.K. & E.A. McFarlane, page 156; Nicholas Meyjes, page 123; Steinar T. Moen, page 69 (bottom); Tracy Morgan, pages 64 (top), 70 (top), 83, 113; Diane Pearce, page 169; Anne Roslin-Williams, pages 11, 16 (bottom), 28, 45, 170, 178; Serafino, page 21; Phil Timmings, pages 13, 18 (top), 22–4, 148–51; Michael Trafford, page 145; and Alan Walker, page 18 (bottom)
Line-drawings by Annette Findlay

Typeset by Footnote Graphics, Warminster, Wilts
Printed and bound by BPC Hazell Books Limited, Aylesbury

Contents

Am. Ch. Chinoe's Eminent Judge CDX (Companion Dog Excellent) with his son Chuzzlewit's MacHeath.

1

History of the Breed

Origins

With a breed such as the English Springer Spaniel a whole book could be devoted to history. Therefore this chapter is aimed at giving you the overall picture of the development of the breed both in its country of origin and in other countries around the world. I do apologise to any country or person who feels that they should have been included and have not. It is simply because of limited space.

The Breed Standard of the English Springer Spaniel states 'Breed is of ancient and pure origins, oldest of the sporting gundogs; original purpose was finding and springing game for the gun.'

It is widely believed that the spaniel came to the UK with the Romans, most probably – as the name would suggest – from Spain. An old law of Wales (AD942) makes reference to spaniels. There are some very interesting manuscripts in the British Museum dating from the reign of Henry IV in which spaniels are praised for the way in which they spring game for hawks and hounds. Possibly the first time that 'Springer' was used to describe these land spaniels was in 1570, when Edward VI's physician Dr Caius, who wrote extensively on the subject of dogs, used this description in his book *De Canis Anglicas*.

In the early 1800s the Boughey family of Aqualate in Shropshire started a distinct strain of spaniel, and from 1813 onwards kept a stud book for what they called their 'Springer Spaniels', this almost a century before the Springer was given separate recognition by the Kennel Club. Towards the end of the nineteenth century great interest was being shown in the working abilities of spaniels. In 1885, the Spaniel Club was formed and breed standards were drawn up for the different types of spaniel.

The first club to run field trials for spaniels was the Sporting Spaniels Club. The first trial was held on the estate of Mr William

Arkwright at Sutton Scarsdale in Derbyshire on 3 January 1899; the club went on to hold a second trial on 12 December 1899 on the estate of Mr B.J. Warwick near Havant in Hampshire. Unfortunately a Springer did not feature in the first three placings at either trial. In these early trials there were often classes, that we do not see today, for brace and team, since spaniels of the time were often worked in this way.

The Spaniel Club ran its first trial in January 1900 at Welbeck Abbey, five years after the Club was established. The judges were Mr J. Farrow and Mr C.A. Phips. This trial was won by a Clumber Spaniel called Beechgrove Bee belonging to Mr Winton Smith. The following year the Club held its second trial and this was won by an English Springer, Mr Gardner's Tring.

In 1903 a separate register in the Stud Book granted sub-divisions for English and Welsh Springer Spaniels, and seventy-five English Springers were registered in that year. Amongst them was Velox Powder, bred by Sir Thomas Boughey and born on 30 July from two unregistered parents, Randle and Bella. The Stud Book shows that, in the ownership of Mr C.C. Eversfield, Powder won a second place in both limit and open classes at Crufts in 1907, and is the first English Springer to be listed in the Stud Book as a champion in the 1910 issue. Ch. Velox Powder is said to have won some twenty field trial stakes, and he was still shown in the listings in 1913, which would mean that he was still winning at ten years of age.

In the very early days the breed could be shown or trialled and in either case gain the title of Champion; but in 1909 the title Field Trial Champion was approved by the Kennel Club, thus discriminating between field and bench. On 10 April 1911 it is recorded that Rivington Sam was born, by Spot (unregistered), out of Rivington Riband, owned and bred by Mr C.A. Phillips. He went on to be the first field trial champion listed in the Stud Book, and as this was shown in the 1914 issue it would suggest that he gained his title at three years of age.

Interestingly, in 1914, ninety English Springers were registered, showing a steady increase in numbers with stock still being registered from unregistered parents.

In 1915, Ranger of Ranscombe was born. He was purchased by Miss Dorothy Moorland Hooper as her first English Springer, and she campaigned him to become one of our best-known early champions. Ranger gained his first Challenge Certificate at Worcester in 1921 under Mr E.C. Spencer. In her book, Miss Hooper recalls,

I won the Limit Class with Ranger and went on to the Open Class, in which were, among others, Mr David MacDonald's Ch. Little Brand from Scotland, another well-known winner. I was placed first with Little Brand second, and I was so astonished that I turned to Mr Spencer and gasped, 'But I haven't beaten Little Brand?' He assured me that I had, and my day was made for me when Mr MacDonald, great sportsman that he was, put out his hand and congratulated me heartily, though I believe that it was the only time his dog was beaten on English soil.

Four years later in 1919 the breed's first dual champion, Horsford Hetman, was born who, I believe, was one of only three dual champions to be made up in the breed in the UK. It is interesting to see how early in registered history these very well-known dogs made their mark. Dual Ch. Horsford Hetman is first mentioned in the Stud Book for his wins in 1921, the year that the English Springer Spaniel Club was founded; that year there were 156 registrations at the Kennel Club.

Austral. Ch. and Ft.Ch. Curtsey George owned originally by Dr. M. M. Wilson and M. L. B. Matthews. George came to the UK and lived with Dorothy Moorland Hooper.

9

The English Springer Spaniel Club was formed as the result of a meeting held at Crufts Dog Show. An application for registration of the title was made to the Kennel Club on 2 April 1921. This was advertised in the April 1921 *Kennel Gazette*, and the application was discussed and agreed at a meeting held in May 1921. The first secretary was Mr William Humphrey, and the committee were described as enthusiastic show and field trial owners.

Dorothy Moorland Hooper was one of the original committee members of the breed club set up at Crufts in 1921 and must have been the longest-serving committee member that the club has ever had as she held this position well into the 1960s. She was very keen on the dual aspect of the breed: her home-bred Rueben of Ranscome gained a Certificate of Merit when handled by Miss Hooper at the very first trial at which either dog or handler competed, while her Rostre of Ranscombe had won an open stake at a field trial and held one CC when the War put an untimely end to her career.

In 1958 the Kennel Club approved the new title of Show Champion. Now dogs could hold the title Champion only if they had won a qualifying certificate at a field trial or at the Show Spaniels Field Day.

Fluctuation in Registration Figures

As the years passed, so the registration figures reflected the increasing popularity of the breed in the UK. There were 608 registrations in 1939: an increase of 452 dogs on the 1921 figure. The figures really took off from then on, and in 1947 there were 3,172 registrations in the Stud Book. Figures dipped during the early 1950s and in 1953 were down to 1,398 for the year. It was 1972 before we saw the figures back up over 3,000. By 1983 figures were up to 6,825, and by 1993 11,148 dogs were registered.

Notable Breeders, 1920s to 1990

Besides the aforementioned, other well-known affixes of this time were Mr A. MacNab Chassels' Inveresk, Mr G.A. Taylor's Carfield, and Mr M.D. and Mr H.S. Lloyd's Ware kennels (famed for both English Springers and Cockers).

The Beauchief affix of Mr Frank Warner Hill was very well known and his dogs were sought after worldwide. Ch. Beauchief Buchanan took the dog CC at Crufts in 1929, Ch. Beauchief Benefactor in 1931 and Ch. Beauchief Boreal in 1939. Benefactor was the first British-bred-and-owned English Springer to win Best in Show at an All-Breeds Championship Show.

Miss Arkwright, a member of the family who arranged the first spaniel field trial, married Major Selby Loundes and they established the well-known Whaddon Chase kennel which was truly dual purpose. After the Second World War Miss Arkwright married again and became Lady Lambe. Her Ch. Whaddon Chase Snipe was well known, and Ch. Whaddon Chase Bonny Tom was thought to have been one of the most influential sires of the 1930s and 1940s.

An influential sire of the 1940s who never gained his title was Boxer of Bramhope, who belonged to Mrs Mary Scott; his best known son was probably Ch. Alexander of Stubham. Mrs Scott was a founder member of the Midland English Springer Spaniel Society, and became its secretary, a post which she held for ten years. In 1958 Mrs Scott judged in the USA and brought back with her Am. Ch. Melilotus Shooting Star from Mrs Gilman Smith's kennel.

Am. Ch. Melilotus Shooting Star, bought from Mrs H. Gilman Smith in the USA by Mrs Mary Scott, who imported Shooting Star to the UK. (See Appendix II where he is included in the pedigree of Sh.Ch. Bella Bee of Kennersleigh, the foundation bitch of Mrs Jean Taylor's Cleavehill kennel.)

Miss C.M. Francis' Higham kennel can boast two full champions who both made it to Best of Breed at Crufts: Ch. Higham Teal was Best of Breed in 1933 and Ch. Higham Topsy in 1955 – quite an achievement. Another truly dual-purpose kennel was the Northdown kennel of Mr W. Manin, while Ch. Northdown Donna won the CC at Crufts in 1958 and 1959. Mr and Mrs D.C. Hannah were known for their Stokeley kennel and took CCs at Crufts with their home-bred champions Bonny Boy, Gay Boy and Lucky; while their Ch. Stokeley Lucky was regularly trialled and was unlucky not to become a dual champion. Another husband and wife team were Mr and Mrs I. Davies who, under their Colmaris affix, bred many champions, including brother and sister George and Contessa who, during 1953 and 1954, took the CCs either singly or both at every Championship Show that they attended. Tragically, George died on the morning of Crufts show in 1955 at only four years of age. He had in his short life won eighteen CCs and ten Reserve CCs, and had been Best of Breed fourteen times.

Mr Michael Withers' Shotton kennels, which were managed by Mrs Gwen Broadley (probably best known for her Labradors) produced Ch. Jess of Shotton, Peter of Shotton and Starshine of Shotton (who later became Mr Joe Braddon's Starshine of Ide), as well as the Int. Ch. Showman of Shotton, who was eventually exported to the USA. Mr Withers gave an English Springer bitch to Mr and Mrs Ian Hampton as a wedding present. This resulted in a new kennel, Larkstoke, being set up (Larkstoke being the area in which the Hamptons were living at the time, near to where Mr Withers lived at Stratford on Avon). Pixie of Larkstoke was the foundation bitch of this successful kennel, and the start of the husband and wife team who became familiar figures in the dog-showing world and still are today.

Mrs Olga Hampton was secretary of the English Springer Spaniel Club for twenty-five years, while husband Ian was treasurer and then chairman. On the death of Mr E. A. Anderson, he took over as president, a post which he still holds today. Their Larkstoke kennel produced two full champions in this country: Ch. Larkstoke Ptarmigan and Ch. Larkstoke Grisette; and six international champions, the best known of whom was Int. Ch. Larkstoke Sarcelle (by Ch. Teesview Tarmac, out of Ch. Larkstoke Ptarmigan). Whelped in 1969, she won Best in Show all breeds at the International Championship Show in Utrecht in 1972 from an entry of 1,500 dogs. The Larkstokes were consistent winners at working tests.

12

Sh.Ch. Douglas of Freetwood owned by Mr A. Stevenson and bred by Mr J. Auld.

Mr and Mrs G.G. Crawford were fortunate enough to start their Winch kennel with the help and advice of Miss Hooper, and were successful through the 1940s, 1950s and 1960s. They made up many champions who were also good workers.

Mrs F.O. Till started her kennel of Stubham English Springers in 1947 and made up many champions and show champions, the best known of whom is probably Ch. Alexander of Stubham. Bred and owned by Mr and Mrs Till he won Best of Breed at Crufts in 1953 and 1960. He was a son of Boxer of Bramhope and out of Susan of Stubham, and won a total of twenty-three CCs. Like his sire he was considered to have made a great impact on the breed as a stud-dog.

The Brandyhole kennel of Mrs J. Spence was also doing well around the same time, and many champions were bred by Mrs Spence. Mr E.A. Anderson's Crosslane kennel combined both show and field trial blood and was successful in the ring – something that is getting increasingly difficult to do today. Mr D.P.B. Campbell

Ch. Studley Diadem owned by Mrs F. O. Till and bred by Mrs S. G. Smithson.

from Scotland was well known in the 1960s and 1970s with his Inverruel affix. Mrs Smithson, with her Studley dogs, made up several champions and show champions. The aforementioned Mrs Broadley ran some English Springers with her well-known kennel of Sandylands Labradors, and owned several champions in the years after the War.

Mrs Joan Dinwoodie bought her first champion English Springer, Banner of Beechfield, as a puppy from Mr Thompson in Yorkshire in 1949, and campaigned him to become a full champion. When she married in 1952 she joined her husband as a partner in the affix Lochar, which was then used on both Labradors and English Springers. Unfortunately, Ch. Banner of Beechfield was poisoned in 1953, but by this time Mrs Dinwoodie was hooked on English Springers, and so the Springer side of the Lochar kennel was founded.

Mrs Dinwoodie bought in two bitches, one from the Conneil kennel of Mrs C. Crawford, who interestingly produced a litter of eight tri-colour puppies. On the death of Mr Dinwoodie his widow transferred the partnership to a very good friend, Mrs Nina Best, and so the partnership still continues today, a small select kennel which has produced several champions over the years.

I feel that I have been most fortunate to have been able to watch two great show Springers make history: the two biggest winners in the show ring in the UK have both come from very similar blood-lines. Firstly Mrs Judith Hancock's and Mr Jimmy Cudworth's Sh.Ch. Hawkhill Connaught was campaigned to win fifty Challenge Certificates. He was Best in Show at seven All-Breed Championship Shows and won fourteen gundog groups, including the group at Crufts in 1974. He sired twenty-four English champions and a further five CC winners, despite retiring from stud at the early age of seven as a result of injury.

'Con' was breed record-holder until recently when his famous relative, Mrs Frances Jackson's Ch. Mompesson Remember Me, took over the title of top-winning English Springer of all time with a total of fifty-four Challenge Certificates to date, and winning three groups along the way. The Hawkhill kennel of Mrs Judith Hancock (later in partnership with the late Mr Jimmy Cudworth, who died unexpectedly on 9 May 1989) was born from a great love of English Springers from a very early age. Mrs Hancock's father was a keen shooting man and when Judith Robinson, as she was then, was only ten years old an English Springer was bought from Mr Arthur Froggatt (father of Ernest Froggatt) called Moorcliff Major. This was the first English Springer of show type to live at Hawkhill. When Miss Robinson left school at the age of fifteen she served an apprenticeship at the well-known kennels of Miss Sedor-ski, and from there went to work at the aforementioned Stubham kennel of Mr and Mrs Till. This seemed a natural progression, as Miss Robinson already owned a Stubham bitch, Starlet of Stubham, who was the foundation bitch for the Hawkhill kennel.

During her teenage years she became a familiar figure in the show ring with her Hawkhill affix rapidly making a name for itself. In 1964, now Mrs Judith Hancock, she was unable to take a most promising young bitch she owned to Crufts and so she asked a friend to take her for her. The bitch was the thirteen-month-old Slayleigh Paulina, and the friend Mr Jimmy Cudworth (who had previously campaigned Ch. Mowgrain Mr Chips to his title). Lady

Lambe was judging at Crufts and awarded Paulina Best of Breed and the bitch CC (the first of twenty-six CCs that she was to win). Jimmy and Judith became partners and Paulina, when mated to Ch. Moorcliff Dougal of Truelindale, produced four puppies in her first litter, three of whom were to become champions. They were: Sh.Ch. Hawkhill Royal Palace, Mr E. Froggatt's Sh.Ch. Hawkhill St Pauli Girl, and Miss Frances Bagshawe's foundation bitch for the Mompesson kennels, Sh.Ch. Hawkhill Derby Daydream. In the next litter from a repeat mating came the great Sh.Ch. Hawkhill Connaught and Mr E. Froggatt's Sh.Ch. Hawkhill Prince Consort of Moorcliff. A further repeat mating produced a sixth champion, Sh.Ch. Hawkhill Happy Memory. This kennel must hold a very special place in the history of show English Springers, having won in the region of 150 CCs over the years and having been responsible for helping many new kennels start with good foundation bitches. In 1976 Albany Fine China honoured Connaught by producing a

Sh.Ch. Hawkhill Connaught, owned by Mrs Judith Hancock and the late Mr Jimmy Cudworth. 'Con' was not only one of the greatest English Springer Spaniel show dogs of all time but also a very influential sire, having sired some twenty six show champions in the UK (see Appendix II for pedigree).

Mrs E. Dobson's Ch. Tyneview Margaret.

limited edition china figure of him, made by the sculptor Mr Neil Campbell, one of which was presented to Mrs Hancock and Mr Cudworth. I'm pleased to say that I also have one.

Another kennel established in the early 1950s and still going strong today is the Teesview kennel of Mrs Ellen Dobson. Her interest in English Springers was encouraged by her late husband George, who liked to work the breed. Mrs Dobson's first champion came from Mr George Scott and was reputedly the runt of the litter. Ch. Tyneview Margaret proved to be a good brood bitch as well as a showgirl and, when mated to Am. Sh.Ch. Stokeley Toreador, produced Ch. Teesview Titus who in turn sired Sh.Ch. Teesview Pandora of Truelindale. Bred by the late Mrs M. Alder and owned and shown by Mrs Dobson, Pandora held the bitch CC breed record for many years, having won thirty-five CCs, and was only beaten recently by Ch. Mompesson Remember Me. Mrs Dobson has continued to make up many champions and continues to breed and show in the 1990s.

Probably the most dual-purpose kennel that we have today would be the Shipden kennel of Colin and Carolyn Muirhead. Established

Ch. Sotherton Phantom of Shipden, owned by Mr and Mrs C. Muirhead and bred by Mr and Mrs B. Smith.

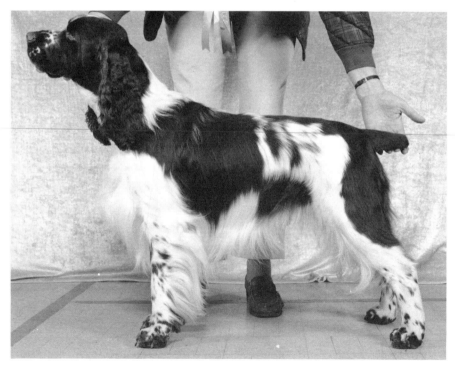

Sh.Ch. Shipden Chuck Berry, owned and bred by Mr and Mrs C. Muirhead.

half a century ago, this kennel is still well known today for producing good show stock who retain their working instincts and are very capable of doing their job on a day's shooting. Their Ch. Swallowtail of Shipden must surely go down as one of the greats, and they are still making up champions today who can trace their ancestry back to him.

The bitch record-holder in the 1950s was Ch. Tillan Toddy, who won fifteen CCs. She was bought by Mr John (Jack) Bolton with work in mind, but proved herself well equipped to make a show dog and a super foundation bitch for the Pencloe kennel. The kennel is still active today with the help of Jack's daughter Morag, who so ably piloted her whippet Ch. Pencloe Dutch Gold to win Best in Show at Crufts in 1992. Through the years this small kennel has owned and bred some seven champions.

The year 1948 saw Mr Ernest Froggatt bringing the Moorcliff kennels to the fore with champions being made up over four decades, firstly by Mr and Mrs Froggatt and later by Mrs Pam

Sh.Ch. Pencloe Miss Chattaway, owned by Miss M. Bolton.

Wadsworth. Mr Froggatt bought the black and white Bramhope Recorder, whom he made up to a full champion and who won the Mary Scott Award for Best Performance by a Show Spaniel at the Midland Field Trial. He feels that the best English Springer he ever owned was Ch. Moorcliff Dougal of Truelindale, who won a total of twenty-two CCs during his career.

Another dual-purpose kennel of the 1950s was the Northdown kennel of Mr W. Manin, his Ch. Northdown Donna winning the CC at Crufts in 1958 and 1959.

In 1949 Mr and Mrs F. George bought an in-whelp bitch from Mr W. Hepplewhite of the Happeedaze kennels. This bitch joined one they already owned, of mostly Beauchief breeding, and together they founded the kennel of Mrs 'Mickie' George that we know today. Her first CC winner came in 1960, but it took until 1988 for Mrs George to make up her first Show Champion Mortondawn Annastasia. A true competitor, she says that she has enjoyed every minute of it.

Another small but successful kennel which started in the late 1940s was Woodbay, of the late Mrs Frances Sherwood who made up Sh.Ch. Woodbay Diane's Dilly, Sh.Ch. Woodbay Prima Donna and Sh.Ch. Woodbay Don Derry herself or in partnership with Mr Manin. Ch. Woodbay Gay Charmer was made up in partnership with Mrs Isobelle Jenkins, and four more Woodbay Springers were made into international champions.

It is impossible to mention all of the kennels here: many made their mark on the breed as it progressed through the years, some lasting longer than others. Miss C.M. Francis' Higham affix was well known in the early days after the War, as was the Whitebrook kennel of Mr and Mrs A. Fowle. Mr and Mrs H. Stewart's Appin dogs can be found in many an old pedigree, as can of course the Truelindale Springers of Miss Madge Alder, whose affix is still used today in Ireland by Mr and Mrs Rickie Hughes on their English Springers and Setters. Mr A.B. Nicholson's Glenbervie affix was well known for his English Springers and Whippets. Mrs Jean Oakey's Eydon affix was truly a mixture of working and show lines. Mrs Beryl Carstairs' Whitemoor kennel produced Sh.Ch. Whitemoor Lady Diane and the two brothers by Connaught, Sh.Ch. Whitemoor Idle Chat and Idle Rich.

Mr and Mrs Jeff Backhouse started the Majeba kennel with a Wire Fox Terrier and, after trying one or two other breeds, bought an English Springer called Blossomtime of Bramhope, who Jeff cam-

Tack du Moulin Quignon, owned by M. Louis Pruvot, Abbeville.

paigned to make up to a champion. When work took Mr and Mrs Backhouse to America Blossomtime went too, and despite only being there about twelve months gained two CCs. This small kennel bred three champions, two campaigned by Mr and Mrs Backhouse, and the third by Mr L. Antcliff. This was a Connaught daughter called Sh.Ch. Majeba Meadow Mint. Mrs Backhouse served as secretary to the Midland English Springer Spaniel Club for some twenty-five years, and jointly the Backhouses were largely responsible for so many people enjoying the show spaniels field day, which was run annually by that club.

Mrs Margaret Keighley bred the brother and sister combination of Sh.Ch. Drummer Boy of Kennersleigh and Sh.Ch. Dulcie of Kennersleigh, who each won eight CCs, the former in the hands of his breeder and the latter with Mrs Jean Taylor, who had already bought from Mrs Keighley Sh.Ch. Bella Bee of Kennersleigh as a puppy, and campaigned her to her title. These two bitches, bought in the early 1960s, were the foundation of the well-known Cleavehill kennel that is still very active today.

21

Mrs Jean Taylor's Sh.Ch. Cleavehill Indian Tree.

Mrs Taylor, the 'home of black and whites', has made up or bred some twenty-five champions over the years, her favourite being Sh.Ch. Cleavehill Corn Dolly. Sh.Ch. Cleavehill Yankee Clipper took the dog CC at Crufts in 1976. He was a grandson of Sh.Ch. Bella Bee of Kennersleigh through Cleavehill Mary Poppins, and by Ch. Teesview Tarmac. In 1982 Mrs Taylor made up both Cleavehill Huckleberry Finn and Cleavehill Johny Walker to show champions. Most recently, Sh.Ch. Cleavehill Bewitched was made up in 1995. Mrs Taylor has been responsible for helping many a newcomer get started with help and advice as well as good foundation bitches.

Another kennel still very active today and started around the same time as Cleavehill is the Feorlig kennel of Mr and Mrs Don Miller. Mr Jack Bolton and his family were old friends of Don and his then fiancée Jenny, and gave them Pencloe Clearway as an engagement present. This little bitch produced four show champions for Mr and Mrs Miller, including the brother and sister combination by Sh.Ch. Hawkhill Connaught, Sh.Ch. Feorlig Golden Griffin and Sh.Ch. Feorlig Golden Gayle. This very successful ken-

Mr and Mrs D. Miller's Sh.Ch. Penygader Chrystal Star.

nel has gone on to produce many show champions including: Sh.Ch. Feorlig Country Classic, who went Best of Breed and reserve in the gundog group at Crufts in 1987; Sh.Ch. Feorlig Van Der Valk, who won the dog CC at Crufts in 1989; and Sh.Ch. Feorlig Life Line, who went Best of Breed at Crufts in 1991.

Mr Bob Jackson (who is now married to Frances, of the Mompesson kennel) started his Romaline kennel with Labradors and bought his first English Springer from Mr and Mrs Froggatt in the late 1960s. He piloted Sh.Ch. Moorcliff Regent to his title and later bought a Connaught daughter Sh.Ch. Moorcliff Sunnymaid. These two were the foundation of the kennel which has gone on to produce some six show champions. Mr Jackson owned the bitch ticket-winner at Crufts in 1985, Sh.Ch. Lyndora Easy Come Easy Go of Romaline, bred by Mrs Dorothy Bury. Mrs Bury herself came to Springers having been showing Dalmatians since the late 1950s, making up one champion along the way. In 1972 she bought from Mr Harry Walmsley a Connaught daughter called Hildarry Roast Chestnut

23

Sh.Ch. Lyndora Beautiful Music, winner of fourteen Challenge Certificates for her owner-breeders Tom and Dorothy Bury.

and made her up to a show champion, taking Best of Breed at Crufts in 1977. From this start the Lyndora kennel has made up or bred eight English Springer Champions, including the 1995 Crufts Best of Breed winner Sh.Ch. Chaun Chablis at Lyndora.

The Mompesson kennel, home of our breed record-holder Ch. Mompesson Remember Me, was started by a very young Miss Frances Bagshawe back in the 1960s. As a small child she had spent many hours at the Hawkhill kennel of Mrs Judith Hancock, and very much as Mrs Hancock went to work for Mr and Mrs Till on leaving school, so Miss Bagshawe went to work for Mrs Hancock. Naturally, the foundation bitch for the Mompesson kennel came from Mrs Hancock. She was Sh.Ch. Hawkhill Derby Daydream, a full sister to Connaught from a previous mating. From Derby Daydream Mrs Frances Cottrell (as she was by then) bred Sh.Ch. Mompesson Wonderful Dream, whom she piloted to Best of Breed and

A UK Breed record-holder with fifty-four Challenge Certificates,
Ch. Mompesson Remember Me, owned and bred by Mrs F. Jackson
(see Appendix II for pedigree).

reserve in the gundog group at Crufts in 1975: quite an achievement
for an owner, breeder and handler of only twenty-one years old.

Including the fifty-four CCs won by Remember Me, the Mompesson kennel has now won well over 100 Challenge Certificates,
the 100th being won on the day that Remember Me beat the bitch
CC record. Mrs Frances Jackson (as she is now) says that the biggest
thrill of all was when she and Remember Me attended the Dukeries

Sh.Ch. Mompesson Proper Charlie with owner and breeder Mrs F. Jackson.

Gundog Club's Field Trial and, under judges Dr N.O. Jones and Mr M. Rock, Remember Me gave a sufficiently good account of herself to win her qualifying certificate. This does prove that the old adage 'you can't teach an old dog new tricks' is not true, as this was her first attempt at her qualifier and she was seven years old!

Another kennel keen on gaining Qualifying Certificates for its dogs is the Cliffhill kennel of Mr and Mrs T. 'Doug' Sheppard. This kennel started in 1973 with a bitch called Silveroak Elaine, purchased from Mr and Mrs Mike Bundy. Mated to Ch. Teesview Titus, Elaine produced Ch. Cliffhill Juliet, and Ch. Cliffhill Julius who won seventeen CCs and sired many champions including my own Ch. Ardencote Alexander and my mother's Sh.Ch. Ardencote August Love, Mr and Mrs Peter Wood's Sh.Ch. Coorigil Charisma, Dr Graham Rogers' Ch. Cliffhill Cavalier of Chaigmarsh, and is grandfather of the same owner's Sh.Ch. Chaigmarsh Sudden Impact. This kennel has bred several champions and has exported many dogs who have gained their titles abroad, amongst them Swed. Int. Ch. Cliffhill Gossips Field Day.

My own Ardencote affix was first used to register a litter of Labradors in 1965, but it was 1973 before I bought my first English Springer, Hawkhill Tranquility, from Mrs J. Hancock. I bought her as a Christmas present for my then fiancé, now husband, but then had her signed over to me after an argument! She was by Sh.Ch. Hawkhill Finlandia, out of a Connaught daughter Teesview Telma, and in her first litter, which resulted from a mating to her grandfather Connaught, she produced for me Sh.Ch. Ardencote Tapestry, who won twelve CCs and fourteen Reserve CCs, and was top-winning English Springer Spaniel bitch in 1978 and 1979. She went on to win Reserve Best in Show at the National Gundog Championship Show and her final Reserve CC at Crufts, both from veteran classes. A repeat mating produced Sh.Ch. Ardencote Autosport, owned by Mrs Linda Barber. Tragically Autosport was killed in a road accident while still quite young. Our small kennel has also bred South Afr. Ch. Ardencote Adventurer, my mother's Sh.Ch. Ardencote August Love and my own Ch. Ardencote Alexander, who has undoubtedly been the character of the kennel. Having been sold as a pet he came back at six months of age because he was too exu-

Sh.Ch. Ardencote Tapestry owned and bred by Mrs J. Wood.

The author's Ch. Ardencote Alexander showing the 'type', following on from his dam Sh.Ch. Ardencote Tapestry.

berant, and that is how he went through life, even to the extent of stealing the next dog's retrieve the day he got his Qualifying Certificate!

The late 1970s became the time of the beautiful bitches. Connaught produced some super dogs but his bitch puppies really stood out. His top-winning daughter was Mr Erik Chadburn's Sh.Ch. Trand Breñ Ragaple who won fifteen CCs. Mrs Barbara Lillie's Sh.Ch. Barlochan Bellringer did a lot of winning and went on to produce Sh.Ch. Barlochan Engineer, who himself went on to sire Sh.Ch. Wadeson the Equalizer. Mr and Mrs Carl Jellicoe's Sh.Ch. Monclare Jennifer Eccles, bred by Mr and Mrs I.J. Sharples, started their Chasmar line.

Sh.Ch. Thornlea Dainty Lady and her brother Sh.Ch. Thornlea Cascade did a lot of winning for the Scottish kennel of Mr G.S. Leckie.

Two younger sisters of my Tranquility bought from the Hawkhill kennel became the foundation bitches for two kennels that were to make their mark on the Springer world. Mr Glen Miller founded his Graftonbury kennel on Sh.Ch. Hawkhill High Society of Lawnwood who, when mated to Sh.Ch. Monclare Mr Chips, produced Sh.Ch. Graftonbury Genghis Khan, who not only proved to be a very good sire but also won Best of Breed and the gundog group at Crufts in 1985. The Robil kennel of Mr and Mrs Ron Billows began with Sh.Ch. Hawkhill Hazy Idea, a start from which they have gone on to produce five show champions to date, and from which Mrs Yvonne Billows found the interest that fired her enthusiasm sufficiently to become the first secretary of the Lancashire and Cheshire English Springer Spaniel Club. Not to be outdone by his sisters, Sh.Ch. Hawkhill High Line, when mated to Sue Shaw's Healsville Waratah Blossom, produced the beautiful Sh.Ch. Windydale Whimsicle Ways of Calvdale, who was a wonderful start for Mrs Nicky Calvert's Calvdale kennel. Whimsicle Ways won twenty-one CCs, sixteen Reserve CCs and was top gundog bitch for 1983.

The first litter of Mr and Mrs John Palmer's Roandew kennel came from a mating between Doravian Bryony and Sh.Ch. Romaline the Amarouse Rascal in 1980, a mating which produced Sh.Ch. Roandew Allanie. This small kennel has gone on to win a total of twenty-two CCs to date, their Sh.Ch. Roandew Gemima Jones having taken two Best in Shows at All-Breed Championship Shows. Mr and Mrs Ron Morris started their Morrivale kennel in the late 1970s with a bitch bred by Mr Morris' brother, called Morrivale Talbot Girl, who was by Healville Digger Boy, out of Breamark Contessa. This bitch and Sh.Ch. Mompesson Pride and Joy are responsible for the successful small kennel that Mr and Mrs Morris have today.

The Wadeson kennel of Mr and Mrs Colin Woodward bought its foundation bitch from the Feorlig kennel of Mr and Mrs Don Miller. She was a daughter of Connaught, out of Feorlig Beautiful Memory, called Feorlig Jus' Jolene. From this start this small kennel has made up seven show champions, amongst them Sh.Ch. Wadeson Miss Marple who has notched up thirty-one CCs, a Reserve Best in Show at WELKS (West of England Ladies' Kennel Society) Championship Show, two groups and two reserve in groups, despite being in the ring at the same time as the breed record-holder. This kennel has also recently made up Sh.Ch. Drakespur Different Strokes who was bred by the very sporting Mrs Jill O'Keefe. Mrs Kay Woodward is now secretary of the Midland English Springer Spaniel Club.

Mr and Mrs C. Woodward's Sh.Ch. Wadeson Miss Marple . . .

. . . and their Sh.Ch. Wadeson the Equalizer.

Mrs Margaret Bower started the very successful Bowswood kennel with Sh.Ch. Woodgill Shadowfax of Bowswood, who was bred by Mr and Mrs Girdwood by Carwinley Cavalcade out of Knightward Leanora. From this start Mrs Bowers, with the help of husband Alan, bred many show champions.

Mr and Mrs Alan Geddes made up Sh.Ch. Debanza I'm in Clover and her son Ch. Debanza Buccaneer during the late 1980s. Mr Colin Jackson, the well known partner of Sh.Ch. Monclare Mr Chips back in the 1970s, has joined forces with Mr and Mrs Tom Aston in the Tasa affix and they have bred one Norwegian and five English champions.

Mr and Mrs Ray Smith have been showing two lovely bitches throughout the late 1980s and early 1990s. Sh.Ch. Chetruda Lancashire Rose of Melverly, bred by Mrs Val Lockhart, and Sh.Ch. Melverly Lois Lane who took Best in Show at the English Springer Spaniel Club Championship Show in 1994 under Mrs Kate Keely.

Mr and Mrs Bob Bentley must have the most successful veteran ever seen in the UK with their black and white Sh.Ch. Wenark Justin Step. Bred by Wendy Bentley he is by Sandale Song n Dance out of Wenark Cornflake. Established in 1977 the Bomaris kennel of Mr and Mrs Dick Sheppard has done very well with one champion being made up in Switzerland and three more in this country, one of whom, Bomaris Envoy to Shipden, then went on to gain his Australian title.

Mrs Fran Glendinning, currently the secretary of the Southern English Springer Spaniel Club, made up an old favourite of mine Sh.Ch. Great Expectations of Plaiglen. A mother and daughter combination, Anne and Dawn Swales have been successful throughout the 1980s with their Sericum kennel. Mrs Ann Corbett, with her Trimere affix, has made up Ch. Trimere Trinity, top-winning bitch of 1983, Sh.Ch. Trimere True Grit and most recently Sh.Ch. Trimere Terrahawk at the Lancashire and Cheshire Club's Championship Show under specialist Mrs Caroline Muirhead.

Mrs Eunice Ward's Sh.Ch. Wardhill Whistling Miller has made his mark not only in the ring but also as a stud-dog. He is home-bred by Sh.Ch. Malacou Dusty Miller out of Sh.Ch. Wardhill Whistling Magic.

This is as comprehensive a synopsis of kennels through the years as space will allow. I do hope that it has enabled you to build in your mind a picture of how our breed has developed through the years.

The Great Divide

By the 1940s and 1950s the 'show' and 'field trial' kennels were becoming quite separate, a fact that depressed many people, but in a quest for winners in both fields the breed became more and more divided. Looking at photographs from the early part of this century it occurs to me that the English type of show English Springer is the nearest to the dogs of that time, with the field trial dogs in the UK and show dogs in the USA having gone to extremes either side of our show dogs. But then perhaps it could be said that I am biased in my opinion!

Having said that, there were only ever three dual champions in our breed in this country. These were: the aforementioned Horsford Hetman, who belonged to Mr William Humphrey; a son of Hetman out of Horsford Ho called Thoughtful of Harting, belonging to Colonel F.H.B. Carrell; and the Duke of Hamilton's Flint of Avendale. It would seem that the early Springer enthusiasts worked their

Ch. Marmion of Marmion owned by The Hon. G. Scott. This dog went back to Ch. Nuthill Dignity on his sire's side and Dual Ch. Flint of Avondale on his dam's side. His stud fee in the early 1930s came to four guineas.

dogs as well as showing them, with one 'type' being bred primarily for looks and the other for working ability and style. With increasing competition over the years it seems inevitable that specialization would produce variations in appearance and type.

The late 1960s and early 1970s saw the formation of a number of Spaniel 'meets', 'get togethers' or 'training clubs', coinciding with there being more leisure time available for would-be handlers as the field trial/working scene changed. Hosted by Mr Peter Moxon, the Midland Spaniel Get Together was one of the first to be set up. It has been successful over the years and is still going strong. Tests were organized initially to gauge the progress of club members. These tests have since developed into a sport at least as big as field trials, with prestigious tests such as the Gundog International at the Country Land Owners' Game Fair, and a whole weekend of gundog tests organized by *Shooting Times* and Pedigree Pet Foods.

In the 1980s the Kennel Club, having monitored the situation for quite a few years, decided, amidst many recriminations, to control gundog working tests, to try and ensure that the demands of tests were kept as similar as possible to the demands of field trials. The aim was to ensure that our gundogs' existing capabilities would be preserved.

At around the same time as the training clubs were being formed, increasing use and availability of cars allowed more people to use what may now, with hindsight, be termed 'over popular' sires. Hales Smutt, although he did not win a field trial, sired many litters and produced many field trial champions. In the mid-1970s Don of Bronton became very popular, as did his son Badgercourt Druid, who sired many litters. Druid's sons Cortman Lane and Courtman Gary both won the Spaniel Championship and were used extensively at stud, as was another son Badgercourt Moss.

The pedigrees of many working spaniels are now much closer than they used to be. Whether this is a good thing remains to be seen.

The Field Trial Kennels

Mr R.R. Kelland was one of the stalwarts of the early Springer world, training his first dog before the turn of the century. He judged in the early days at both field trials and shows, but his interest lay in the field trial side of the breed. He joined the English

Springer Spaniel Club in 1924 and served as secretary, chairman and president over a period of thirty years. Very well known throughout the field trial world during the 1920s and 1930s was Mr G. Clark's Blair kennel. His bitch F.T.Ch. Bee of Blair was a wonderful worker and the dam of innumerable field trial winners. If you could trace your pedigrees back far enough you would find her behind many of today's dogs.

The O'Vara kennel of Mr Selwyn Jones and Mr T.J. Greatorex was famed for its field trial winners, making up some seventeen champions, amongst whom F.T.Ch. Scramble O'Vara won the Kennel Club Spaniel Championships twice. A very well-known trainer of gundogs, Mr Andrew Wylie, started his Pinehawk kennels in 1933, and this name is still familiar to many today. Mr J. Chudley and his brother Mr K. Chudley started training at their Harpersbrook kennels in 1946 and have trained and competed with many successful Springers since. Mr P.R.A. Moxon is well known not only for his training of gundogs, but also for the books he writes on the subject. Mr Tom Laird from Scotland has been very successful with his Criffel dogs, making up several F.T. Champions since the War. At over eighty years of age, Mr Danny McKenzie is still going strong with his Staxigoe field trial dogs, his most notable litter probably being the one that produced F.T.Ch. Staxigoe Swing, F.T.Ch. Staxigoe Shimmer and F.T.Ch. Staxigoe Swank.

In the 1950s Keith Earlinson started with Major Spittle's Dinas Dewi Sele, the first of many F.T. Champions he has handled; Cortman Lane is the most recent. Major Spittle was, of course, field trial secretary of the English Springer Spaniel Club for a great many years. Another who started around this time was Mr Frank Bell, with his Adee's Shineradee and Slideradee. Mrs Rachel Gosling produced many Parkmaple dogs, of whom F.T.Ch. Parkmaple Jolly, handled by Mr E. Roberston, won both the Kennel Club Championship and the Irish Championship in the same season.

The Markdown affix of Mr F. Thomas has produced some very good winners, the best known of whom is probably F.T.Ch. Markdown Muffin who, trained and handled by Mr John McQueen, came second in the Spaniel Championships in 1961 and won them in 1962. Mr John McQueen moved to the Rytex kennels of Mr R.F. Naylor, producing F.T.Ch. Rytex Rex in 1969. In the early 1980s Mr Ian Oppenshaw took over Mr Naylor's kennels from John McQueen, quickly coming out with the outstanding bitch F.T.Ch. Rytex Ria, who so nearly won the Spaniel Championships on two or three occasions. He has produced a number of F.T. Champions and in the 1994/95 Championships qualified five dogs. He won the Championships in 1990/91 with F.T.Ch. Rytex Racine, in 1992/93 with F.T.Ch. Poppet of Bolscote, and in 1993/94 with F.T.Ch. Kennine Tina.

In the late 1960s Mr Harry Hardwicke, who is chairman of both the Kennel Club Field Trial Committee and the Spaniel Club, owned and trained F.T.Ch. Lenstan Paul, the first of seven F.T. Champions he has produced. At about the same time Mr Bill Bremner produced F.T.Ch. Superscot Scamper, F.T.Ch. Staxigoe Skimmer, F.T.Ch. Concraig Bess and F.T.Ch. Burnhatch Pimms.

Between 1970 and 1975 Mr Tim Healey produced F.T.Ch. Farway Shann, F.T.Ch. Farway Skipper and F.T.Ch. Farway Mac, and bred F.T.Ch. Don of Bronton who, trained and handled by Mr Con Lloyd, won his title after competing in only four field trials.

Mr C. Lawton Evans has won the Kennel Club Spaniel Championships five times. He won the 1970/71 season with F.T.Ch. Coppicewood Carla, the 1971/72 season with F.T.Ch. Robbie of Barnacre, both the 1974/75 and 1975/76 seasons with F.T.Ch. Sport of Roffey and the 1977/78 season with Cleo of Coppicewood; quite an achievement.

Other kennels of note since the War have been Dr Tom Davidson's Jonkit, Mr Bernard Dutton's Hamers, Mr Talbot Radcliffe's Saightons, who have had a very strong influence in the USA, Dr Diana Bovill's Barnacle and Mr W. Charles Williams' Berrystead.

The 1994/95 Championships were won by Mr S. Morris' F.T.Ch. Sunny Brae Siskin, who was bred by Mr Keiron Davies and handled by Mr Jim Clark. Looking at the kennels over the years it would seem that many of the large kennels of field trial dogs have on the whole disappeared and we are seeing a new generation of 'owner, handler, trainers', who have just a few dogs for their own pleasure.

Eire

After the War Mr Bob Cleland's Ch. Grand Black Rod (a son of Boxer of Bramhope) was a big winner both in England and Ireland. In 1949 he was top CC-winning dog in the UK, with Mr Bob Gardnier's Ch. Cavehill Maid top CC-winning bitch (both resided in Ireland). Mr Cleland also sold to Mr Joe Braddon a dog called Stand Back, whose name was then changed to Invader of Ide and who won a total of twenty-five CCs; a breed record until overtaken by Sh.Ch. Slayleigh Paulina.

Another dog to win well on both sides of the Irish Sea was Int. Ch. Print of Ardrick owned by Mr Burton. This son of Ch. Clintonhouse George was Best of Breed at Crufts in 1958 under Mrs Mary Scott. Print also proved himself an excellent sire: his most famous son was probably Mr Jim Cranston's Int. Ch. Sir Knight, who in turn sired Mr Mervyn White's Ch. Duke of Cleevaun. The latter was a very big winner in Ireland in the 1960s, winning many groups and taking Best in Show at the Royal Dublin Society Championship Show. Mr Knight went on to have further success with Ch. Knight of Cleevaun. Mrs Bernie Ladd had great success with Kennersleigh Moonraker, a bitch imported from Mrs Margaret Keighley, and with the home-bred Corrlough Crystal Clear and Corrlough Corrie Doon.

The well-known Chevalaux kennel of Mr and Mrs Pat Dineen had its first big winner in Ch. Ravensbrook Regent, a son of Ch. Duke of Cleevaun, who was bred by Mrs Elizabeth Davin. They then imported Glad Rags of Shipden and, mated to Int. Ch. Sotherton Phantom of Shipden, she produced Ch. Chevalaux Huntress and Peadar Crowley's Ch. Chevalaux Gladness of Remington. When Chevalaux Glad Rags was mated to Ch. Moorcliff Dougal of Truelindale her litter produced two champions: Ch. Chevalaux Cavaleer and Int. Ch. Chevalaux Crown Prince. The O'Dwyer family have had many winners over the years and made up Ch. Graffin Melody. Probably the best-known exhibit to have come from the Mirah kennel of the Quinlands from Kerry is Ch. Mirah Eider.

One of the top-winning Springers of all time in Ireland was Eng. Sh.Ch. Remington Rockin Red Wing, a son of Ch. Chevalaux Cavaleer and Ch. Chevalaux Gladness of Remington. He was a multiple Championship Show group-winner as well as winning Best in Show and Reserve Best in Show at Championship Shows. Remy was bred by Peadar Crowley and owned by Mr and Mrs Rickie Hughes who themselves bred Windyacres Heir Apparent, later to be exported to Australia to become an Australian Champion. Also in their kennel was Cleavehill Beauvalet, the top winner in the breed in 1986. The star of the kennel, however, was English Sh.Ch. Skelsea Amber Solaire, the winner of five CCs and reserve in the gundog group at the Border Union Championship Show. Although not bred by Mrs Taylor she was all Cleavehill breeding, being by Sh.Ch. Cleavehill Johnie Walker, out of Cleavehill Chelsea Girl. The English Springers owned and showed by Rickie Hughes did not gain their Irish titles

36

A big winner in Ireland and England, Sh.Ch. Remington Rockin Red Wing, owned by Mr and Mrs R. Hughes and bred by Mr P. Crowley.

despite winning many, many green stars between them, as they never competed for their qualifying certificates in the field, which prior to 1990 it was necessary to have before becoming a champion. In 1990 the Irish Kennel Club introduced the title Show Champion for Gundogs Not Holding their Qualifying Certificate.

Six dogs have gained their Show Champion titles since 1990. The Belview kennel of Heather Cox and Ruth Jackson have two of them: Ir. Sh.Ch. Morrivale Poppycox and Ir. Sh.Ch. Belview Bithne O'Reilly. David Murphy also has two: Ir. Sh.Ch. Mompesson Masterpiece and Ir. Sh.Ch. Mompesson Just Remember. Graham and Caroline Osborne's Sh.Ch. and Ir. Sh.Ch. Beaters Brigadoon, and Liz Portlock's Ir. Sh.Ch. Carmis It's a Delight are the others.

USA

It is believed that a spaniel brought on the *Mayflower* landed at Cape Cod in the early 1600s. This was not of course any particular variety of spaniel as at this time no separate classifications of spaniel were recognized.

In the late 1800s the differentiation between Cockers and Springers was recognized. The American Spaniel Club was founded in 1881 and, as in England, the spaniels started to be divided by weight. It is reported that two Springer Spaniels were exported to America in 1907, but there is no record available in the USA of these dogs being bred from. In 1910, a bitch named Denne Lucy was the first Springer to be registered with the American Kennel Club.

The English Springer Spaniel Field Trial Association was set up in America in 1922 by Mr S.G. Allen, Messrs W.H. and A. Ferguson, and Mr W. Hutchenson (owner of the Horsford kennels in England), who also acted as advisor. In 1927 the American Kennel Club recognized this club and shortly afterwards regulations, standards and trials were established, modelled on their English counterparts.

The first show to classify English Springer Spaniels was held at Madison Square Gardens, New York, in 1923, followed one year later by the first field trial, which was run at Fisher Island. First place was taken by Aughrim Flash and second by Horsford Hale, both imports from Great Britain.

Eudore Chevrier of the Avandale kennel in Winnipeg imported many English Springers from England after he acquired a dog, who greatly impressed him, called Don Juan of Gerwn. Mr Chevrier had taken Don Juan in to his boarding kennels in 1914, from his owner Mr W.H. Gardner who had purchased the dog at Crufts from Col. A.T. Williams of North Wales. Don Juan had been competing in field trials in the UK prior to his export, and Mr Chevrier was very taken with the dog and his working abilities.

One of the most influential of his early imports was Can. Ch. Springbok of Ware, who was purchased from Mr H.S. Lloyd in 1922. He typified the dual-purpose dogs of the day and would not be out of place in the show ring today. He is described in *The English Springer Spaniel in North America* (*see* Bibliography) as close to the modern ideal, standing 21in to the top of the shoulder and weighing about 55lb. It states that he was a big dog, yet not coarse, and not larger than the present Standard stipulates.

Kennels were being established all over the USA with stock brought over from England. Over on the west coast Mr and Mrs C.H. Jackson's Blue Leader kennels had many good imported dogs while, also in California, Ernest Leffingwell imported Eng. Am. Ch. Nuthill Dignity, a dog who strongly resembled Int. Ch. Dry Toast.

Ch. Dry Toast, a big winner in the UK between the Wars, who could hold his own in the ring today.

Dorothy Moorland Hooper said of Dignity, 'he completely satisfies me as a typical and beautiful Springer, which yet looks capable of a good job of work, as I know he was. I wish we had more like him now.' I must say that from looking at his photograph I am inclined to agree with Miss Hooper; let us hope that we are producing dogs today that will be as well thought of in seventy years' time.

The first English Springer to become a bench Champion in the USA was bred by William Humphrey from Shropshire, and belonged to Dr A.C. Gifford of the Winnebago kennels near Wisconsin. She was Horsford Highness, a daughter of English Dual Ch. Horsford Hetman. Fifteen other bench titles were won by Horsford dogs during the next four years.

A very highly thought-of sire was F.T.Ch. Rex of Avendale (not to be confused with Eudore Chevrier's Avandale affix), and many dogs were exported to the USA from the Duke of Hamilton's Avendale Kennels in Scotland.

Dorothy Moorland Hooper states,

In the years between the two World Wars many of the best of our English Springers of both show and working strains travelled to the United States and Canada from such kennels as the Rivington, O'Vara, Banchory, Denne, Avandale, Inveresk, Ware, Cairnies, L'ile Rufton and Saighton.

The greatest influence in the 1930s is thought to have been Eng. Am. Ch. Rufton Recorder. An amazing number of his progeny were exported to Canada and the US before eventually Mr and Mrs Fred Hunt of the Green Valley kennels brought Recorder himself over to America; and even though he was about eight years old he gained his American title.

In 1938 Mr Billy Lang introduced a new affix to the US with the import of Eng. Am. Ch. Showman of Shotton, purchased from Mr M.D. Withers on behalf of Mr P.Q. Quay of Ohio. Ably handled by Billy Lang, Showman became an English, American and Canadian Champion. It must have been quite something to travel all those miles before transport became as convenient as we know it today.

As early as the 1930s dual-purpose dogs were becoming fewer and fewer, and the 'great divide' between bench and field was widening both in the USA and the UK. One of the best-remembered imports of the 1930s in the field trial world was Eng. Ind. Am. F.T.Ch. Wakes Wager of Greenfair, who must have enjoyed travelling, as he gained his title in England, India and America! Wager was bred by Mr F.M. Prime in England and, after he had been sold to a Maharajah in India, Mr J.C. Quirk took him to America where he left his mark with six champion offspring. Interestingly, down from his line came some winners on the bench, despite any bench winners on his own pedigree being some six generations back.

The breed's working abilities were greatly publicized during the 1930s and 1940s, and the Springer became a very popular sporting dog, with many field trial clubs being formed.

The Second World War saw a drastic reduction in the number of British dogs being imported into the USA; although the field trial and working fanciers were still importing some stock.

Many of the original kennels did not continue after the War. A new kennel to spring to the fore, however, was the Sandblown Acre kennels of William Bellville. He had been showing successfully throughout the late 1930s and he applied some of the principles he used as a plant geneticist to produce a glamorous line of English Springers who seem to have started the pattern for show Springers in America today. Am. Ch. Rodrique of Sandblown Acre was the dog whom Mr Bellville chose to be the mainstay of his breeding policy. He sired some twenty-eight champions, and appears many times in the pedigrees of Mr Bellville's dogs, where father-to-daughter and then back-to-grandfather-type matings were common, with Rodrique as the sire.

The kennel that was to have the greatest influence on the show English Springer Spaniel in America was founded in the 1930s and is still to the fore today, some sixty years later. Mrs Julia Gasow's Salilyn affix is known all over the world. She was named 'Dog Woman of the Year' in 1971 and 1980, and 'Breeder of the Year' in 1970 and 1975. Her Am. Ch. Salilyn's Condor is the top-winning English Springer Spaniel of all time and number one sporting dog in history in the USA. However, it is generally thought that the dog to have had the greatest influence from Mrs Gasow's kennel is Am. Ch. Salilyn's Aristocrat, sired by Am. Ch. Inchidony Prince Charming, out of Am. Ch. Salilyn's Lily of the Valley and whelped on 19 December 1964. Not only did he sire 188 champions himself, but many of his sons and grandsons went on to sire champions. He won forty-five Best in Shows in one year and his show record was only to be shattered by one of his sons, Am. Ch. Chinoe's Adamant James, the most influential show Springer of the 1970s.

Another kennel of the 1930s that should not pass without note is that of Mr Charles Toy, whose Clarion kennels were situated about sixty miles from Pittsburgh. Mr R.E. Allen of Provo, Utah, had a kennel housing many champions at this time. Probably the best known was Ch. Timpanogos Melinda, who won the group at Westminster in 1942. Melinda was a predominantly white bitch with heavy ticking; very different to what we see in the ring in the USA today. Mrs Gasow wrote in *The New Complete English Springer Spaniel* that 'The dogs generally, were longer in body than our present Springer. They were short on legs with poor fronts. Most were heavily ticked.' From the pictures of the time they seem more closely to resemble the English Springer Spaniel show dog as seen in the UK than the ones seen in the USA today.

By the 1950s there were some thirty field trial clubs holding competitions and the two 'types' of English Springer were quite evident. The field trial supporters were still bringing fresh stock in from the UK but it was rare for show stock to be imported. In fact

A well known champion in the USA in the 1960s, Canarch Inchidony Sparkler, owned by Mary Lee Hendee. (See Appendix II: breeding included in pedigree of 'Soft Music'.)

only three dogs were brought in during the 1950s: Studley Hercules, Glencora Countryman and Rosthern Hunter. They were little used, and only Glencora Countryman gained his title, although Rosthern Hunter can be found in the pedigrees of dogs noted for their smooth reaching gait.

Through the late 1950s and early 1960s Mrs Gasow's name crops up again with her Am. Ch. Salilyn's Macduff being top-winning English Springer Spaniel in the USA in 1958, 1959 and 1960. In the early 1960s Juanita Howard's Am. Ch. Waiterock Elmer Brown took this award in three consecutive years, whilst Anne Pope's Am. Ch. Charlyle's Fair Warning took it twice. Anne Pope's Felicia affix combined old New England show lines with those of Salilyn.

Am. Ch. Chinoe's Adamant James made his presence felt strongly in the early 1970s and he made history when he won Best in Show at the Westminster Kennel Club in both 1971 and 1972. Interestingly, top-winning sporting dog in the late 1970s was Am. Ch. Salilyn's Hallmark, whose great-grandmother, Am. Ch. Kennersleigh

Cleavehill Beliza Bee, was imported from the UK. The first English bitch to be made up in the USA since the War, she was bred by Mrs Jean Taylor in Yorkshire and was sent to Mary J. Hosteney in California by Mrs Margaret Keighley.

A most important sire of the late 1970s and early 1980s was Delores Stuart's Am. Ch. Telltale Author. He was an Aristocrat son and was the sire of more than seventy-five champions, fourteen of them produced by matings between him and Am. Ch. Stepney's Cinderella, and one of them being the great Am. Ch. Telltale Royal Stuart. This dog became top-winning English Springer Spaniel in USA history when he won his sixty-seventh All-Breeds Best in Show award in 1989. In 1981 and 1982 the top winner again carried the Salilyn affix. This time it was Am. Ch. Private Stock who took the top honours, owned jointly by Robert Gough and Julia Gasow. Another multiple winner of this award was Am. Ch. Jester's 'Lil Limerick, who took the award in 1987 and 1988.

Am. Ch. Salilyn's Condor has dominated the early part of the 1990s as the top-winning English Springer Spaniel of all time in the USA.

The English Springer Spaniels in the USA today are shown and presented very differently to their counterparts in the UK, and this has led to comments being made that the dogs shown in these two countries appear so different that they seem to be different breeds. This is not what either country wishes to happen, and liaison between the parent breed clubs in both countries is aiming to improve this situation.

The field trial-bred English Springer Spaniels represent a different type of dog again. As you will have seen throughout this chapter, the breed has been developed for its different requirements. There is still much UK stock being imported into the USA for field trial work from such kennels as Saighton, Brickclose. Windmillwood, Badgercourt, Housty, Cortman, Gwibernant, Gorsty and Rytex. The work required of the dogs is somewhat different to the work required in the UK (*see* Chapter 6).

Australia

The *Sun Dog Book*, published in Melbourne in the 1930s, reported that English Springer Spaniels had been imported to Tasmania prior to 1914. John Peters, in his research into the history of the English

Springer Spaniel in Australia, found references to these dogs and their descendants in pedigrees, registration certificates, catalogues and canine magazines.

In the late 1920s and early 1930s there were quite a number of English Springer kennels in Tasmania, such as: Mowbray, Franklin, Wentworth, Donibrook, Leith and Everton. There was also the Mortyn, from where Mr O.R. Gourlay of South Yarra, Victoria, purchased Mortyn Jack O'Hearts who was born in 1930, and the Rev. N.T. McDonald of Quambatook, Victoria purchased Mortyn Jack and Mortyn Jill in 1931 and 1932. So, we see the first documented evidence of English Springer Spaniels living on the Australian mainland.

Beauchief Punch appears to be the first English Springer to have been exhibited at the Melbourne Royal. This was in 1933, one year before Springers were given their own classification. Punch was from a litter conceived in England, out of Beauchief Belle and by Ch. Beauchief Buchanan. Mr H.C. Little of the Bocara kennels, Hobart, Tasmania purchased Belle and Bocara from Mr F. Warner Hill. Although these two dogs had the Beauchief affix they were not bred by Mr Warner Hill, but were bought in and sold on to Mr Little. Bocara was formerly Lune Jock, bred by a Mrs Harvey, and Belle was bred by a Mrs Duckering. It would appear that in those early days the Kennel Club rules on names and registrations were somewhat different to those of today.

After the War increasing interest was being shown in English Springers for work, and stock was brought into Australia from the UK and from New Zealand. In 1947 Mr Frank Martlew brought in from New Zealand the dogs Hugo and Importance of Ardencote (no connection with my affix), and he shot over these dogs regularly. Bessie of Bramhope was exported to Australia at around this time, in whelp to Boxer of Bramhope, and two puppies from the resulting litter, Scawfell Lady and Scawfell Prince, were among the early dogs in the Edenfield kennel of Mr R. Langford.

In 1948 the first show classes to be held at the Sydney Royal especially for Springers were judged by Mr A.G. Nichols from England. In the early 1950s Mrs Helen Sapio moved her Cruchfield kennel from New Zealand to Queensland, Australia. She was to have a great influence on the English Springer in Australia, through both her home-bred dogs and her many imports who included: Strathblane Renown, Sir Echo of Chastleton, Strathblane Warspite, Higham Tobit, Strathblane Garganey, Sh.Ch. Moorcliff Wigeon and

*Sh.Ch. Moorcliff Freetwood Gamecock, owned by Mr Ernest Froggatt
and exported by him to Australia.*

Majeba Mystery, all from England; and Am. Ch. Dr Primrose of
Wakefield, from the USA.

Mr B. Nelson of the Oak kennels in South Australia brought into
the country from England Sh.Ch. Moorcliff Freetwood Gamecock
and Moorcliff Pintail, who was nursing a litter by Ch. Moorcliff
Dougal of Truelindale by the time they landed on Australian soil.
Some of the resulting progeny from these imports helped start the
Cranloch kennel of John and Lily Tulloch in Victoria, Stephanie and
David Rickard's Wongan kennel, also in Victoria, Marie and Phil
Merchant's Clanach kennel in South Australia, and May and John
Peters' Drumhill kennel in New South Wales. Gamecock won nine-
teen CCs in England whilst owned by Mr Ernest Froggatt and was un-
beaten in breed classes in Australia taking eight Best in Show awards.

45

Another very successful import of the 1960s was Miss Marjorie Morris' Scottann Samson, whom she brought over from England in 1965. He was Best of Breed at Brisbane Royal in 1965, 1966 and 1967, Best in Show winner and, at the age of ten, he took the reserve CC to his son at the first ever Australian Springer Speciality.

During the 1970s Mrs Holland of the Adroch kennel imported from Mrs Farrell of the USA Hilrays Avant Garde and Hilrays Aurora. Mrs R. Tissington brought in Special Edition of Cleavehill, and Mrs Tissington, Mrs Walker and Mr and Mrs Cheetham brought in Cleavehill Heilan Eriskay from the Cleavehill kennel of Mrs Jean Taylor at Thirsk in Yorkshire.

Moving towards the 1980s there were several kennels who looked to England for new stock, notably the Wongan kennel of Mr and Mrs D. Rickard, who brought in Ch. Mompesson Sleeping Partner, Mompesson Midsummer Lad, Monclare Sugar 'n' Spice and Hawk-hill Crepello. The Drumhill kennel of Mr and Mrs J. Peters imported Sh.Ch. Chasmar Penny Farthing of Moorcliff, in whelp to Sh.Ch.

Austral. Ch. Casa Perez Dona, owned by Mrs R. Holland.

46

Thornlea Cascade, and Ch. Moorcliff Kalico, and the Clanach kennel of Mr and Mrs R. Merchant purchased Hawkhill One in a Million, in whelp to Sh.Ch. Graftonbury Genghis Khan. These imports all brought to Australia a strong influence of the Hawkhill kennel of Mrs Judith Hancock, many of them being closely related to the famous Sh.Ch. Hawkhill Connaught, who was co-owned by Mrs Judith Hancock and Mr Jimmy Cudworth, and was campaigned by Mr Cudworth to become breed record-holder for a very long time, with fifty CCs won under different judges. In fact Connaught is currently top-winning male English Springer Spaniel of all time.

Field Trial Dogs in Australia

Victoria is the major centre for field trials in Australia. The leading kennel in this discipline is Wrangham, belonging to Miss Rachel Greaves, who has had a great deal of success with both home-bred and imported stock.

Miss Greaves has kindly written the following for me:

Undoubtedly the biggest influence on the working Springer scene in the last thirty years was my acquisition of Bellever Raffleson from Rupert Hill in 1979. His breeding was by F.T.Ch. Crowhill Raffle out of F.T.Ch. Nell of Bellever, both winners of the UK Spaniel Championship (he was a Hales Smut grandson, she a Hales Smut great-granddaughter). When Raffle won his first trial in Australia it was the first time for sixteen years that a spaniel had won a trial in Victoria (the most active trialling State). Since that time English Springer Spaniels related to Raffleson have won over two-thirds of the trials held in Victoria, as well as all three National events. He also sired two litters in New Zealand and those dogs (in particular Ger. F.T.Ch. Bee of Sirah-Selah) have also been big winners and have changed the face of trialling in that country too.

Other Spaniels I have imported who have been used to improve the field trial breeding have been the bitches Cuchullin Beag, Crowhill Floss and Glencaol Farway Sine, and the dog Glencaol Farway Rory. Lynley Fox-Cumming in New South Wales imported two bitches, Kirtdon Minstral and GolliGoch Tessa (who arrived in whelp to Cortman Lane). Jerry Cole has a bitch, Glencaol Farway Sari, and the late Trevor Carter in Tasmania had a few dogs from Pinehawk kennels.

Miss Greaves goes on to say that she has made good use of the dogs imported in to New Zealand and that stock often goes to and fro

47

between her kennel and New Zealand. In fact one of her best-performing bitches (a Raffleson daughter), F.T.Ch. Marny of Sirah-Selah was born in New Zealand.

So, a reasonable pool of good, talented dogs is maintained, all of whom have good stamina, an attribute essential in Australian conditions.

Norway
(By Ellen Getz Wold and Heidi Fosberg)

The history of the English Springer Spaniel in Norway began in 1948, when Ch. Sandylands Showgirl (then mated to Sandylands Shrubby) came to Norway from England. In the 1950s and 1960s there were very few litters, but in the late 1970s a few breeders started breeding Springers. Ch. Silveroak Ysenne was imported to the kennel Travis, and her daughter Ch. Travis Aelia came to be the foundation bitch of the kennel Inn-Goya. This kennel has so far

Int. and Nor. Ch. Brigadoon Scarlet's Nimblewit.

produced fifty-two champions from three different Spaniel breeds, which makes it the leading Springer kennel in Norway.

Various English kennels have influenced the development of the breed in Norway over the last fifteen years including: Cleavehill, Teesview, Wenark, Freeway, Coorigil, Shalloway, Melverly, Wadeson and Chaigmarsh.

Numbers of English Springers in Norway are still quite small with 150–200 registrations per year; while in Sweden there are approximately 1,000–1,100 registrations per year. We have frequently co-operated with Sweden in our breeding, and the top-winning English Springer of all time is Swedish bred, this being Int. Norw. Sh.Ch. Brigadoon Scarlets Nimblewhit, Norwegian Winner in 1991 and 1993. This bitch has won thirty Best of Breed awards in Norway and Sweden and she was Best in Show 3 (third in the BIS line-up) at the Norwegian All-Breed Championship Show in Oslo in June 1994.

At the Nordic Winnershow in December 1994, the young bitch,

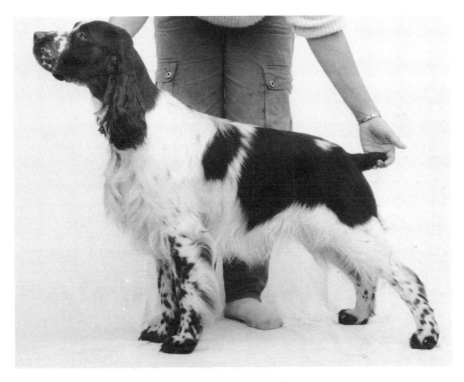

Int. Nor. and Fin. Ch. Brigadoon New Generation of York.

Norw. Dan. Sh.Ch. Whisborne Rule Britannia, was Best of Breed, Best in Group and Best in Show 2 (Reserve). She is a granddaughter of Int. Norw. Sh.Ch. Melverly Uptown Girl (Best in Show at this show was Eng. Sh.Ch. Chaigmarsh Orshid), bred by the Ulla Larsson's kennel Rowntree, which is one of the top-winning kennels in Sweden.

The numbers of Spaniels participating in field trials are constantly increasing. Today we have several Springers who have received merits in the field, the most successful of them all being Streamside's Blue Quill, a Norwegian-bred bitch who is now a Swedish F.T.Ch.

The future of our breed in Norway looks bright with a few very enthusiastic breeders. The soundness of the breed is regarded as important: all breeding stock is eye-tested and hip-scored. In Norway the Springer has a variety of jobs besides performing in the show ring. Hunters use them not only for hunting, but also for tracking wounded large game. The Police use Springers to search for drugs and bombs. The most important quality of the Springer is, in Norway as it is elsewhere, that he is a gentle, all-round family dog.

Sweden
(By Sigrun Wallguist)

At the beginning of this century there were very few English Springers in Sweden, and these were mainly of German origin. In 1930 a litter was born out of an imported English bitch, mated before her exportation to Shot of Landermere.

In the late 1940s, Mr Stig Onnerfelt, who owned the kennel at Bjerkefall, imported Miss Greta of Ware and Carnfield Craftsman from England, Ch. Petersborgs Peggy (of pure English origin) from Norway, and Ch. Timpanogos Adonis, Timpanogos Anita, Am. Can. Ch. Frejex Royal Minstrel and Frejax Royal Suzette from the USA. These imports helped to get the breed off to a good start in Sweden and there were an increasing number of registrations; about 150 to 200 more each year (all puppies are normally registered in The Swedish Kennel Club). At the end of 1950 the registration numbers went down again as Mr Onnerfelt had more or less stopped his breeding. In 1958, only thirty-eight dogs were registered. However, interest in the breed began to grow again, and in 1960 there

Swed. F.T.Ch. Streamside's Blue Quill (by Swed. F.T.Ch. Klovstamon's S-Pelé, out of Brigadoon Scarlet's Beliza Bee).

began a new era. In 1961 there were two new imports: Ch. Ambridge Bystander of Stubham came to kennel Mustela, and Northdown Donnetta was brought in to kennel Brigadoon. These imports were followed by others from Wollburn, Whaddon Chase, Woodbay, Larkstoke, Bramhope, Hawkhill, Cleavehill, Skilleigh and, later on, a few others from other well known English breeders.

These, together with what was left of earlier imports, produced beautiful, intelligent dogs who also did very well in the field, many of them becoming Dual Champions.

In 1970, and in larger numbers in 1980, the American type of Springer was brought in from Finland and the USA (the American dogs being purely of show stock). Nearly all were imported by newcomers to the breed, these being mainly former Cocker breeders, who started to create a smaller, more upstanding, compact type. At this time Sweden also got a group of new judges who found this new type very attractive. The group was populated largely by intelligent people, who were able to take on the theoretical aspects of the breed very quickly, but who did not have Springer-breeding experience. Many of them had never seen a Springer pup grow into

51

Int. and Swed. Ch. Rowntree Magic Touch.

a youngster, mature and become a fully grown beautiful Springer of the correct English type. Regardless of this, their success in the show ring helped registration numbers to rise to 1,000 and above each year.

A number of dogs of working type were also imported, almost all of these coming to shooting people in the south of Sweden. Breeders also tried to mix dual-purpose dogs with American types, and they also added working lines. Their goals were probably to create a nice-looking Springer with more working ability.

Currently it looks as if there may be a turning point towards the English type of Springer again, but the ability to import dual-purpose dogs seems to have gone for ever. As with many other breeds, newcomers have brought both good and bad to the breed. The difficulty is to see that a Springer Spaniel is in fact far from being just a gigantic Cocker Spaniel – that is a completely different breed, even if they were connected in ancient times.

It is difficult to mention notable breeders, as there will surely be someone forgotten. One of the oldest breeders, however, is kennel Brigadoon which started in 1963 and has so far produced seventy-one champions all over Europe, and among these dual champions. Kennel Beeline, kennel Springstar, kennel Aimpoint, kennel Gofield, kennel Hallagarden and younger kennels, such as Rowntree, Winner Ghost and Whisborne have all produced champions. There are also, of course, even younger kennels that have just begun, some of which will produce good Springers for the future.

Over the years Sweden has also shared breeding experience and stud-dogs, with excellent results with Norway, Finland and, to a smaller extent, with Denmark.

2

The Breed Standards

The Breed Standard as laid down by the Kennel Club is the blueprint to which we breed and judge in the UK. The Federation Cynologique Internationale instructs all judges officiating in member countries that they should judge according to the Breed Standard of the country of origin. In the USA the breed is judged to a slightly different and far more concise Standard. When read carefully these slight differences become apparent and explain why the English Springer that we see in the show ring in the USA varies somewhat from the English Springer that we see in the show ring in the UK

The UK Standard for the breed was first approved by the English Springer Spaniel Club of England, the Spaniel Club of England, the English Springer Spaniel Club of Scotland and the Spaniel Club of Scotland on 16 May 1934 and further revised in April 1969. The Kennel Club of England first published the Breed Standard in 1949. They subsequently took over responsibility for all breed standards from the relevant breed clubs in 1982, and now hold copyright on them. For the purposes of comparison, the UK Breed Standard of 1934 is reproduced in Appendix I.

The Kennel Club published an illustrated book of breed standards in 1989. By this time they had standardized and shortened many of them and, in doing so, had lost a lot of the more descriptive content. I will therefore endeavour to explain the Standard further on in this chapter.

The English Springer Spaniel falls within the Gundog Group at Kennel Club shows, along with the Cocker Spaniel, the Field Spaniel, the Sussex Spaniel, the Clumber Spaniel, the Welsh Springer Spaniel and the Irish Water Spaniel.

The UK Breed Standard
(Reproduced by kind permission of the Kennel Club)

General Appearance

Symmetrically built, compact, strong, merry, active. Highest on leg and raciest in build of all British land Spaniels.

Characteristics

Breed is of ancient and pure origins, oldest of sporting gundogs; original purpose was finding and springing game for net, falcon or greyhound. Now used to find, flush and retrieve game for gun.

Temperament

Friendly, happy disposition, biddable. Timidity or aggression highly undesirable.

Head and Skull

Skull of medium length, fairly broad, slightly rounded, rising from foreface, making a brow or stop, dividing by fluting between eyes, dying away along forehead towards occipital bone which should not be prominent. Cheeks flat. Foreface of proportionate length to skull, fairly broad and deep, well chiselled below eyes, fairly deep and square in flew. Nostrils well developed.

Eyes

Medium size, almond shaped, not prominent nor sunken, well set in (not showing haw), alert, kind expression. Dark hazel. Light eyes undesirable.

Ears

Lobular, good length and width, fairly close to head, set in line with eye. Nicely feathered.

Mouth

Jaws strong, with a perfect, regular and complete scissor bite, i.e. upper teeth closely overlapping lower teeth and set square to the jaws.

55

Neck

Good length, strong and muscular, free from throatiness, slightly arched, tapering towards head.

Forequarters

Forelegs straight and well boned. Shoulders sloping and well laid. Elbows set well to body. Strong flexible pasterns.

Body

Strong, neither too long nor too short. Chest deep, well developed. Well sprung ribs. Loin muscular, strong with slight arch and well coupled.

Hindquarters

Hindlegs well let down. Stifles and hocks moderately bent. Thighs broad, muscular, well developed. Coarse hocks undesirable.

Feet

Tight, compact, well rounded, with strong full pads.

Tail

Set low, never carried above level of back. Well feathered with lively action. Customarily docked.

Gait/Movement

Strictly his own. Forelegs swing straight forward from shoulder, throwing feet well forward in an easy free manner. Hocks driving well under body, following in line with forelegs. At slow movement may have a pacing stride typical of this breed.

Coat

Close, straight and weather resisting, never coarse. Moderate feathering on ears, forelegs, body and hindquarters.

Colour

Liver and white, black and white, or either of these colours with tan markings.

Size

Approximate height 51cm (20in).

Faults

Any departure from the foregoing points should be considered a fault and the seriousness with which the fault should be regarded should be in exact proportion to its degree.

Note

Male animals should have two apparently normal testicles fully descended into the scrotum.

Interpreting the Standard

As a preface to the Standard the Kennel Club's book states,

> The name, Springer, is derived from the use of this type of Spaniel to startle the birds into the air so that they spring upwards. The English Springer, with his black and white or liver and white markings is the traditional dog for the rough-shooter – a dog capable of working tirelessly all day; ready to enter water even when he has to break ice to do it. Like so many of the gundog breeds, his cheerful extrovert nature has endeared him to the general public, and he is in great demand as an energetic companion for a growing family. His thick coat is tough and weather-resistant, but like so many spaniels his lengthy ear flaps need to be kept well-trimmed if he is not to suffer from uninvited seeds and twigs getting inside the more sensitive depths of the ears themselves.

I would add to this foreword that the breed has developed along different lines for its different purposes, and that the majority of the dogs found working for their living now do not have such heavy feather and large earflaps as the dogs bred for show purposes, and therefore are not so inclined to get tangled up in briars.

General Appearance

The Standard calls for the English Springer to be symmetrically built. Symmetry is described in the dictionary as 'commensurate, due proportion of the several parts of a body or any whole to each other, congruity, parity, regularity, harmony; arrangement of parts on either side of a dividing line or point so that opposite parts are exactly similar in shape and size; regularity of structure so that opposite halves exactly correspond.' I think that the best way to describe an English Springer from that interpretation would be with the word 'harmony'. The picture that gives us is of a balanced dog in harmony with itself; a dog not quite elegant, but as elegant as a practical working dog can be. The Standard goes on to call for 'compact, strong, merry, active, and highest on leg and raciest of British land Spaniels'. A difficult combination, compact though racy, and yet it works in an English Springer. These Spaniels should never be cloddy or coarse but they must be workmanlike with the heart and lung room to give them the stamina to work a long day in tiring conditions.

Characteristics and Temperament

The very fact that the English Springer is a working gundog means that his character is one of a biddable, friendly fellow, happy to mix with other dogs and happy in the company of humans. Having said this they can be self-willed and destructive, particularly when young, and do require a firm hand and some form of training. When at work or in the show ring they should always be bold and friendly, and any form of nervousness or aggression is totally atypical.

Head and Skull

This is a most important part of the English Springer: the first thing that takes your eye on meeting a dog is his head. It should be well chiselled, as though carved from stone, without being too exaggerated. The bone structure of the head should be almost apparent, but not to the extent of the bones protruding or there appearing to

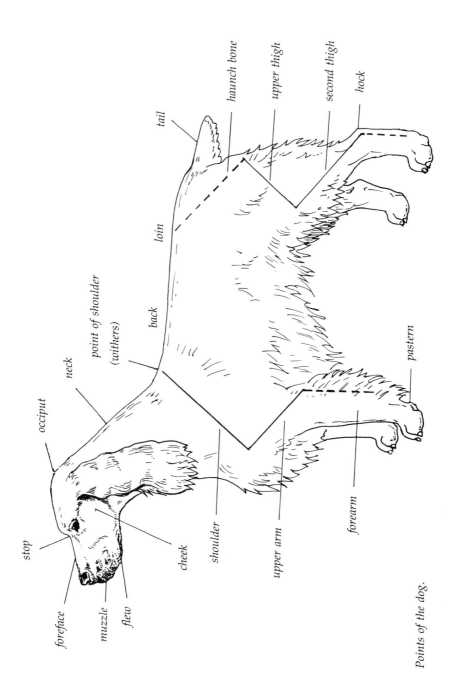

Points of the dog.

59

be hollows above and below the eyes. The foreface should be of equal length to the length of skull, it should be moderately broad and deep, providing the strength for retrieving a large cock pheasant or hare. The flew should be fairly deep and square, covering the teeth and gums to protect them from briars and brambles. Shortage of flew gives a snipey, collie-like appearance, and is most undesirable. The nose is black and should be well pigmented, not showing any pink. The nostrils should be well developed. The eyes should have a delightful, soft and yet intelligent expression, sometimes a little questioning. Their colour should tone with the body colour: dark hazel eyes with a liver and white or liver, white and tan coat; and black or almost black with a black and white or black, white and tan coat. Light eyes are most unattractive and detract greatly from the desired expression, although they are slightly more acceptable in a very young dog whose eyes have a dark outer rim, as this usually means that the eyes will darken with age. The eyes should be of medium size, almond-shaped and set into the head neither too deep nor protruding. There should be no sign of wetness or lack of pigment on the eye-rim. A loose eye-rim known as 'showing haw' is most undesirable as it is not only unattractive but leaves the eye open to injury and the entry of grass seeds. There should be a moderate stop between the eyes, and then a gentle rise in a slight groove from that stop, finishing short of the occipital bone, which should never be prominent. The skull should be fairly broad, very slightly rounded, never coarse or domed, with the ears set on to the sides of the skull, level with the eyes. The ears should be lobular and of fair width, with length of leather (earflap) reaching the nose when pulled forward. They should be well feathered and lie flat against the sides of the head.

The overall appearance of the head should be of quality and balance combined with strength; the toplines of the skull and foreface should lie in parallel planes and the head should be in balance with the rest of the body.

Mouth

The teeth should be of an adequate size for the dog and fit well in his mouth. They should be set squarely to the jaws with the top teeth closely overlapping the bottom teeth in what is known as a scissor bite. It is believed that this type of bite allows the dog to have a 'soft' mouth, which is required for retrieving game. It is said that an undershot jaw, in which the bottom teeth protrude in front of the top teeth, makes for a 'hard' mouth. An undershot mouth, a wry mouth, an overshot mouth, a mouth showing a level bite, or a mouth with some teeth out of line are all incorrect and would be penalized in the show ring.

Neck

The Standard calls for the neck to be of 'good length', necessary to reach for the retrieve; for it to be 'strong and muscular', equally necessary for the dog to carry a heavy cock pheasant or hare; 'free from throatiness', apart from the fact that loose skin looks unattractive, excessive loose skin could be prone to getting caught on branches and undergrowth; 'slightly arched, tapering towards head', this seems to me merely to describe what a strong and muscular neck should look like, as a weak neck would tend to be a 'ewe neck', which would also look unattractive. The length of the neck should be approximately the same as the length of the head and it should flow smoothly into the shoulders. Although the show dog and the working dog may now look quite different, when reading this part of the Standard one can see the reasoning for the original draft.

Ewe neck.   Throatiness.

61

Forequarters

The forelegs should be straight and well boned without being coarse. The bone should not be round and heavy, neither should it be light and weak. The elbows should be placed directly below the point of the shoulder, set well into the body without being so tight as to turn the feet out. The pasterns should be strong and flexible, with dew-claws removed. The upper arm should be of equal length to the shoulder blade, which should be flat and lay smoothly within the structure of the dog. The shoulder blade and upper arm should meet at an angle of 90 degrees thus bringing the front legs well under the body and allowing for the great freedom of movement that should be typical of this breed.

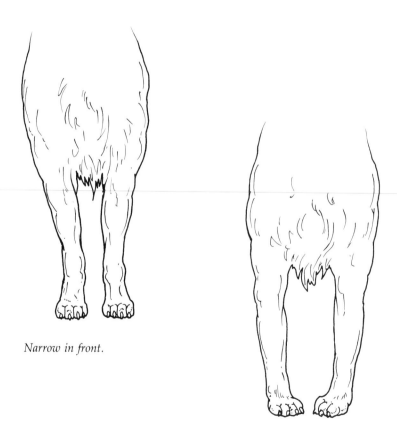

Narrow in front.

Pigeon-toed. If seen like this on the move, said to be 'pinning in'.

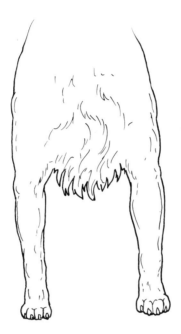

Wide in front.

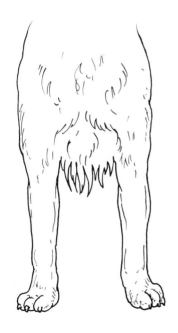

Standing at 'five to one'.

63

Mrs A. M. Corbett's Sh.Ch. Trimere Terrahawk showing a fine example of a well bodied dog.

Body

The body should be strong and well balanced, being neither too long nor too short, although a little extra length is forgiven in a bitch. The chest should be deep and well developed, reaching down to the elbow, with ribs well sprung, allowing for plenty of heart and lung room. Having said this, a barrel chest is equally as undesirable as slab sides. The loin should be strong, well coupled and muscular. The topline should flow from the head down to the point of the shoulders, straight along the back with a slight rise over the loin and dipping slightly over the croup to the set of the tail.

Good quarters.

Hindquarters

This is where the propulsion comes from and it is therefore very important that the hindquarters are strong and muscular. The thighs should be broad and well developed, the hocks well let down and never coarse, and the stifles moderately bent with the angulation of the rear assembly matching that of the forequarters as closely as possible. The hocks should be parallel when viewed from behind and should be set slightly further apart than the front legs when standing, moving in to line with the front legs when on the move. Sickle hocks, cowhocks, lack of second thigh, over-angulation or under-angulation are all equally undesirable as they all produce weakness. If there are hind dew-claws, these should be removed.

Feet

The feet should be tight, well rounded and compact with strong, full, thick pads. The foot should be very much a continuation of the leg and not too much bigger. The toes should be well arched and

65

Cow hocked.

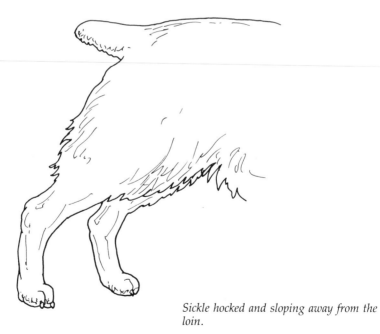

Sickle hocked and sloping away from the loin.

Straight in stifle, long from hock to ground, and too narrow in second thigh.

Overangulated quarters.

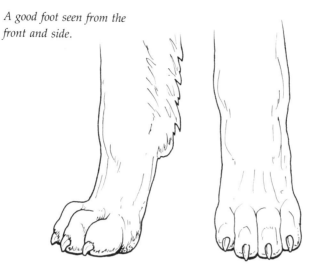

A good foot seen from the front and side.

nails kept trimmed. The feather between the toes helps to give protection when working. A large, open foot is prone to injury as well as looking unattractive, while flat feet are inclined to get the toes knocked up, and a hare foot will tend to make a dog walk on his heels.

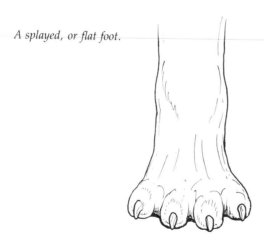

A splayed, or flat foot.

Tail

The tail is set on slightly low and should never be carried above the level of the dog's back. Having said that it should not be set on so

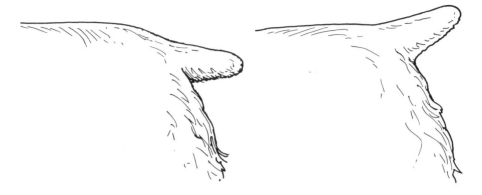

A good tail set.   *Tail set too high.*

low that it gives the impression of the dog crouching. The Standard calls for it to be well feathered, which it would normally be, although it is customary to trim this feather off for the show ring. It is usual for the tail to be docked. The English Springer shows his happy, extrovert character by the lively action of his tail, and in my opinion it is as bad to see a dog with his tail tucked down as it is one that is showing a gay tail.

Nord. Ch. V-94 Whisborne Rule Britannia owned by Annika Ulltviet-Moe and Jessie Madsen, Denmark. A fine example of an undocked dog winning in the show ring.

Mr and Mrs Don Miller's tricolour Sh.Ch. Feorlig Life Line, showing the tan points on his black and white colouring.

TMORGAN.

Gait/Movement

This is a joy to behold and strictly his own: a Springer moving correctly swings his forelegs straight forward from the shoulder, throwing his feet well forward in an easy, free manner. A short, choppy stride is not only unattractive but atypical. His hocks should drive well under the body, with his hindfeet touching the ground in front of the imprints left by his front feet and following in line with the forelegs. At slow movement he may pace, which is typical of this breed; this is where the nearside front and rear legs move forward together, and then the offside legs move forward together. It is most unattractive and a difficult habit to break. When moving faster than desired it may be that the hindlegs will converge, thus bringing them inwards from the track of the forelegs. When viewed in profile the Springer should maintain his topline on the move, and should be seen to cover a great deal of ground with a free, easy

70

stride. When viewed from in front or behind, the forelegs and hind-legs should be parallel, neither turning in nor out. The correct balance and angulation of the forequarters and hindquarters is essential to achieve this overall picture.

Coat

The coat should be close, straight and weather resistant, with a good undercoat to ensure that even in the worst of weather con-ditions the dog does not get cold and wet through to the skin. It should never be coarse or curly, although it is sometimes a little wavy. Moderate feathering is to be found on the ears, the lower part of the body and chest, down the throat, on the back of the front legs, around the inside and back of the hindlegs and quarters and, as mentioned previously, between the toes.

Colour

There are four colours found in English Springers in the UK. These are liver and white, black and white, and either of these colours with tan, then referred to as liver and white tricolour and black and white tricolour. The tan is normally found on the eyebrows, on the inside of the ears, the cheeks, under the tail, and amongst the ticking on the lower part of the legs. It may not necessarily be in all of these places and the quantity of tan does vary from dog to dog. The degree of ticking also varies but it is most uncommon in this country for dogs to have no ticking at all. It is also rare for them to have so much ticking as to appear roan.

Size

The Breed Standard gives the approximate height as 20in (51cm). No allowance is made for any variance in height between dogs and bitches, but most judges would allow for the male exhibits at a show to be approximately 1in taller than the female exhibits. Where in the past few years oversize has been a problem in our show rings, I do feel that breeders are now getting on top of that problem, and exhibits are falling much more in line with the Standard. Equally, a few years ago, field trial exhibits were becoming very small but now seem to be coming back up in size.

71

Faults

The Standard is clear that any departure from the foregoing points should be considered a fault and the seriousness with which the fault should be regarded should be in exact proportion to its degree. What is not so clear is the note that 'male animals should have two apparently normal testicles fully descended into the scrotum'. The Kennel Club have in fact changed their ruling regarding the showing of spayed bitches and castrated dogs, and do now allow such animals to be shown. Therefore, it could quite possibly be that a dog could appear in the ring with no testicles. What is more, no proof of the reason for this is required although the Kennel Club do appreciate being notified by the owner of any dog or bitch having had this operation so that they can note it on the animal's records. Having said that, I have never yet judged a dog with no testicles and doubt that I ever shall do so.

The American Breed Standard provides a far more detailed description of the English Springer than does the UK Standard. For the purposes of comparison, and, it is hoped, to add further substance to the notes that have gone before, the American Standard is reproduced here. There are some slight differences between the two standards, which explain to some extent the differences between dogs shown in the UK and those in America.

The American Breed Standard
(Reproduced by kind permission of the American Kennel Club)

General Appearance

The English Springer Spaniel is a medium-sized sporting dog, with a compact body and a docked tail. His coat is moderately long, with feathering on his legs, ears, chest and brisket. His pendulous ears, soft gentle expression, sturdy build and friendly wagging tail proclaim him unmistakably a member of the ancient family of Spaniels. He is above all a well-proportioned dog, free from exaggeration, nicely balanced in every part. His carriage is proud and upstanding, body deep, legs strong and muscular, with enough length to carry him with ease. Taken as a whole, the English Springer Spaniel suggests power, endurance and agility. He looks the part of a dog that can go, and keep going, under difficult hunting conditions. At

Am. and Can. Ch. Canarch Dark Passage CD, owned and handled by Francie Nelson. 'Dash' was eight years old when this picture was taken and had by then sired some nineteen champions from just six bitches.

his best, he is endowed with style, symmetry, balance and enthusiasm, and is every inch a sporting dog of distinct spaniel character, combining beauty and utility.

Size, Proportion, Substance

The Springer is built to cover rough ground with agility and reasonable speed. His structure suggests the capacity for endurance. He is to be kept to medium size. Ideal height at the shoulder for dogs is 20 inches; for bitches, it is 19 inches. Those more than one inch under or over the breed ideal are to be faulted. A 20 inch dog, well-proportioned and in good condition, will weigh approximately 50 pounds; a 19 inch bitch will weigh approximately 40 pounds. The length of the body (measured from point of shoulder to point of buttocks) is slightly greater than the height at the withers. The dog too long in body, especially when long in the loin, tires easily and lacks the compact outline characteristic of the breed. A dog too short in body for the length of his legs, a condition which destroys balance and restricts gait, is equally undesirable. A Springer with correct substance appears well-knit and sturdy with good bone, however, he is never coarse or ponderous.

Head

The head is impressive without being heavy. Its beauty lies in a combination of strength and refinement. It is important that its size and proportion be in balance with the rest of the dog. Viewed in profile, the head appears approximately the same length as the neck and blends with the body in substance. The stop, eyebrows and chiselling of the bony structure around the eye sockets contribute to the Springer's beautiful and characteristic expression, which is alert, kindly and trusting. The eyes, more than any other feature, are the essence of the Springer's appeal. Correct size, shape, placement and color influence expression and attractiveness. The eyes are of medium size and oval in shape, set rather well-apart and fairly deep in their sockets. The color of the iris harmonizes with the color of the coat, preferably dark hazel in the liver and white dogs and black or deep brown in the black and white dogs. Eyerims are fully pigmented and match the coat in color. Lids are tight with little or no haw showing. Eyes that are small, round or protruding, as well as eyes that are yellow or brassy in color, are highly undesirable. Ears are long and fairly wide, hanging close to the cheeks with no tendency to stand up or out. The ear leather is thin and approximately long enough to reach the tip of the nose. Correct ear set is on a level with the eye and not too far back on the skull. The skull is medium length and fairly broad, flat on top and slightly rounded at the sides and back. The occiput bone is inconspicuous. As the skull rises from the foreface, it makes a stop, divided by a groove, or fluting, between the eyes. The groove disappears as it reaches the middle of the forehead. The amount of stop is moderate. It must not be a pronounced feature; rather it is a subtle rise where the muzzle joins the upper head. It is emphasized by the groove and by the position and shape of the eyebrows, which are well-developed. The muzzle is approximately the same length as the skull and one half the width of the skull. Viewed in profile, the toplines of the skull and muzzle lie in approximately parallel planes. The nasal bone is straight, with no inclination downward toward the tip of the nose, the latter giving an undesirable downfaced look. Neither is the nasal bone concave, resulting in a 'dish-faced' profile; nor convex, giving the dog a Roman nose. The cheeks are flat, and the face is well-chiselled under the eyes. Jaws are of sufficient length to allow the dog to carry game easily: fairly square, lean and strong. The upper lips come down full and rather square to cover the line of the lower jaw, however, the lips are never pendulous or exaggerated. The nose is fully-pigmented, liver or black in color, depending on the color of the coat. The nostrils are well-opened and broad. Teeth are strong, clean, of good size and ideally meet in a close scissors bite. An even bite or one or two incisors slightly out of line are minor faults. Undershot, overshot and wry jaws are serious faults and are to be severely penalized.

Neck, Topline and Body

The neck is moderately long, muscular, clean and slightly arched at the crest. It blends gradually and smoothly into sloping shoulders. The portion of the topline from withers to tail is firm and slopes very gently. The body is short-coupled, strong and compact. The chest is deep, reaching the level of the elbows, with well-developed forechest; however, it is not so wide or round as to interfere with the action of the front legs. Ribs are fairly long, springing gradually to the middle of the body, then tapering as they approach the end of the ribbed section. The underline stays level with the elbows to a slight upcurve at the flank. The back is straight, strong and essentially level. Loins are strong, short and slightly arched. Hips are nicely-rounded, blending smoothly into the hind legs. The croup slopes gently to the set of the tail, and tail-set follows the natural line of the croup. The tail is carried horizontally or slightly elevated and displays a characteristic lively, merry action, particularly when the dog is on game. A clamped tail (indicating timidity or undependable temperament) is to be faulted, as is a tail carried at a right angle to the backline in Terrier fashion.

Forequarters

Efficient movement in front calls for proper forequarter assembly. The shoulder blades are flat and fairly close together at the tips, molding smoothly into the contour of the body. Ideally, when measured from the top of the withers to the point of the shoulder to the elbow, the shoulder blade and upper arm are of apparent equal length, forming an angle of nearly 90 degrees; this sets the front legs well under the body and places the elbows directly beneath the tips of the shoulder blades. Elbows lie close to the body. Forelegs are straight with the same degree of size continuing to the foot. Bone is strong, slightly flattened, not too round or too heavy. Pasterns are short, strong and slightly sloping with no suggestion of weakness. Dewclaws are usually removed. Feet are round or slightly oval. They are compact and well-arched, of medium size with thick pads, and well-feathered between the toes.

Hindquarters

The Springer should be worked and shown in hard, muscular condition with well-developed hips and thighs. His whole rear assembly suggests strength and driving power. Thighs are broad and muscular. Stifle joints are strong. For functional efficiency, the angulation of the hindquarter is never greater than that of the forequarter, and not appreciably less. The hock joints are somewhat rounded, not small and sharp in contour. Rear pasterns are short (about ⅓ the distance from the hip joint to the foot) and strong, with good bone. When viewed from behind, the rear pasterns are parallel. Dewclaws are usually removed. The feet are the same as in front, except that they are smaller and often more compact.

Coat

The Springer has an outer coat and an undercoat. On the body, the outer coat is of medium length, flat or wavy, and is easily distinguishable from the undercoat, which is short, soft and dense. The quantity of undercoat is affected by climate and season. When in combination, outer coat and undercoat serve to make the dog substantially waterproof, weatherproof and thornproof. On ears, chest, legs and belly the Springer is nicely furnished with a fringe of feathering of moderate length and heaviness. On the head, front of the forelegs, and below the hock joints on the front of the hind legs, the hair is short and fine. The coat has the clean, glossy, 'live' appearance indicative of good health. It is legitimate to trim about the head, ears, neck and feet, to remove dead undercoat, and to thin and shorten excess feathering as required to enhance a smart, functional appearance. The tail may be trimmed, or well fringed with wavy feathering. Above all, the appearance should be natural. Overtrimming, especially the body coat, or any chopped, barbered or artificial effect is to be penalized in the show ring, as is excessive feathering that destroys the clean outline desirable in a sporting dog. Correct quality and condition of coat is to take precedence over quantity of coat.

Color

All the following combinations of colors and markings are equally acceptable:
(1) Black or liver with white markings or predominantly white with black or liver markings; (2) Blue or liver roan; (3) Tricolor: black and white or liver and white with tan markings, usually found on eyebrows, cheeks, inside of ears and under the tail. Any white portion of the coat may be flecked with ticking. Off colors such as lemon, red or orange are not to place.

Gait

The final test of the Springer's conformation and soundness is proper movement. Balance is a prerequisite to good movement. The front and rear assemblies must be equivalent in angulation and muscular development for the gait to be smooth and effortless. Shoulders which are well laid-back to permit a long stride are just as essential as the excellent rear quarters that provide driving power. Seen from the side, the Springer exhibits a long, ground-covering stride and carries a firm back, with no tendency to dip, roach or roll from side to side. From the front, the legs swing forward in a free and easy manner. Elbows have free action from the shoulders, and the legs show no tendency to cross or interfere. From behind, the rear legs reach well under the body, following on a line with the forelegs. As speed increases, there is a natural tendency for the legs to converge toward a center line of travel. Movement faults include high-stepping, wasted motion; short, choppy stride; crabbing; and moving with the feet wide, the latter giving roll or swing to the body.

Temperament

The typical Springer is friendly, eager to please, quick to learn and willing to obey. Such traits are conducive to tractability, which is essential for appropriate handler control in the field. In the show ring, he should exhibit poise and attentiveness and permit himself to be examined by the judge without resentment or cringing. Aggression toward people and aggression toward other dogs is not in keeping with sporting dog character and purpose and is not acceptable. Excessive timidity, with due allowance for puppies and novice exhibits, is to be equally penalized.

Summary

In evaluating the English Springer Spaniel, the overall picture is a primary consideration. One should look for *type*, which includes general appearance and outline, and also for *soundness*, which includes movement and temperament. Inasmuch as the dog with a smooth easy gait must be reasonably sound and well-balanced, he is to be highly regarded, however, not to the extent of forgiving him for not looking like an English Springer Spaniel. An atypical dog, too short or long in leg length or foreign in head or expression, may move well, but he is not to be preferred over a good all-round specimen that has a minor fault in movement. It must be remembered that the English Springer Spaniel is first and foremost a sporting dog of the Spaniel family, and he must *look, behave* and *move* in character.

Approved February 1994

3

Choosing your Companion

This is undoubtedly the most important decision you will have to make about your future companion. Be it for show, work or pet, choosing the best breed, type, sex and age for your requirements is essential if you are to enjoy the next thirteen or fourteen years together.

The Kennel Club (*see* Useful Addresses) will give you the name and address of the breed club secretary. A letter or chat on the telephone will fill you in on the general characteristics of the breed. Many breed clubs have information packs which they are only too pleased to send to you, and they normally keep a register of puppies for sale.

Do remember that appealing puppies grow up, in the case of English Springers into energetic, mischievous dogs that will give you hours of pleasure provided you give them plenty of time and affection. They are not dogs for the faint-hearted, but they are the most delightful breed as long as you have the time for them.

People sometimes ask me whether it would be all right to keep an English Springer in the town or city. In my opinion it is not where you keep the dog that counts, but how you look after him. They do not mind where they live provided they have companionship, food, exercise and lots of attention.

Do try to see as many dogs as possible before you finally decide that this is the breed for you. If you want a Springer as a pet, visit a local show, talk to the exhibitors and their dogs. You may not want a show dog but this will give you an idea of their size and coat. You can discuss diet, grooming and exercise requirements. Go and see a breeder; even if they do not have puppies for sale most responsible breeders are only too happy to show people round and discuss the breed.

If you are looking for a dog to show or work, be it for shooting over or for field trials, then you will have to decide not only if this is the breed for you, but which line or type you want to start with.

This can be a far more difficult decision even than deciding on the breed, with so many different avenues to explore. My advice to you would be to take your time, visit as many shows or trials as you can, talk to competitors, or rather let them talk to you, use this time to learn about the breed and to see how things are done in whichever field you have chosen.

Dog or Bitch?

When you have decided that this is the breed for you the question of sex comes into the equation: dog or bitch? Personally I find dogs more rewarding companions that bitches in this breed. I would not say this of every breed, but with the delightful temperament of the English Springer one should not have to worry about male dominance. With a bitch as a pet the twice-yearly problem of seasons can be a bother; not only does it cause a mess in the house and the brown patches that a bitch's urine tends to leave on the lawn, but she may also attract unwanted attention from male dogs in the area. A bitch can be spayed of course, but I have found that this can cause them to get rather fat and sometimes turn a nice smooth, silky coat into a woolly mass. Should sexuality become a problem with a male Springer, castration is a much smaller operation and tends not to have the side effects of spaying and, with patience, it is possible to teach him not to cock his leg on the herbs and vegetables.

If you are planning to start competing with your English Springer, then of course your requirements are somewhat different. It may be that you wish to start showing but not breeding, in which case I would be just as happy to take on a dog as a bitch. If, however, you are wanting to start your own line and breed on, then a bitch is the obvious choice as you can take your bitch to a top-class stud-dog and thus hope to improve on what you have. The likelihood of your first dog turning out to be top class, and therefore attracting a top-class bitch to him for stud purposes, is fairly slim. Occasionally someone is lucky enough to acquire a top-class puppy, rear and school it on properly and make it up to champion, but this is rare.

For working and trialling, opinions vary on the subject of working a dog versus a bitch and, yet again, the breeding-on aspect must be considered. The likelihood of going to the top with your first field trial Springer would be even slimmer than with your first show

Springer, so if you are wanting to breed on then a well-bred bitch would seem to be the best choice.

Puppy or Adult Dog?

Having settled on breed and sex the next step is age: do you want a puppy straight from the nest or something slightly older?

One should consider the length of time that the dog will be your responsibility. Will you still want to be going for long walks in five, six or seven years' time? If not, perhaps you should consider taking on a slightly older dog. There is an excellent English Springer Spaniel Welfare (*see* Useful Addresses). If that does not appeal you will often find that breeders have an older bitch who has bred a couple of litters and would now love a warm hearth to curl up on, or a young dog or bitch that has started its showing career but not made the grade.

Some rather younger members of the breed!

81

If you want a show dog it may be that you would prefer not to take a baby puppy, but one that is several months old, so that you feel you have a better chance of seeing what you are getting. This does not always follow, though, as puppies go through 'ugly duckling' stages. I was told a very long time ago to assess my puppies at four days, four weeks and four months. Others I know like to see them at six weeks and others at twelve weeks. It can be very confusing, but I think you will find that most good breeders know their own stock and will do their best to guide you towards the best choice, whatever age you are looking for. After all, it is their reputation at stake when you turn up in the ring with your young hopeful.

The decision on age is even more difficult to take if you want a dog to work. Do you take a baby and hope that you can teach it yourself? I think probably not with your first English Springer, but, again, be advised by a reputable breeder; by now you should have done sufficient research to know several. It is possible to buy trained or partly trained dogs at varying ages and stages and it would seem sensible to take a dog or bitch who has at least had basic training and is showing aptitude.

Where to Buy From

Now you know exactly what you want, all you have to do is find it! Perhaps along the way you have decided just where the Springer is to come from. If not, another phone call or letter to the breed club secretary in your area could put you in touch with a litter, or your vet may know of a litter in the area. The dog press and local papers sometimes carry advertisements, but do be sure that all the necessary health checks have been done on the parents (*see* Chapter 11).

When to Buy

Before planning this addition to your family consider when your next holiday is going to be. Some breeders will take a puppy back for a week or two rather than have him confused by too many moves early in life, but it is preferable for the puppy to have a few uninterrupted months prior to the confusion of what must seem to him like another new home. It is also worth considering whether

English Springers make wonderful companions for children provided that both child and dog grow up understanding and respecting each other.

there will be anyone readily available to dog-sit for the odd night, should you want to take a weekend away. Boarding kennels have wonderful facilities but many are reluctant to take puppies. Once your dog is older he will probably be quite content to go on his holidays when you go on yours; in fact, many seem to treat their boarding kennels as second homes, settling in really well as soon as their owners have gone.

How to Choose Your Puppy

So now we should be at the viewing puppies stage. It is ideal to be able to see both parents, but this is not always practical. It should not be a problem for you to see the mother and, if possible, any relevant health certificates for her, and possibly copies of the father's. Most breeders like to keep their puppies quiet until after their eyes have opened. Personally I do not like mine to be looked at until they are at least four weeks old: apart from the fact that it can distress the bitch to have strangers staring at her new babies, there is not really much to see before they are four weeks old and starting to get about.

You can expect to be sprayed with a disinfectant to minimize the risk of infection, and some breeders do not like to have their puppies handled. If you are allowed to touch as well as look at this stage, be gentle and if you have children with you please do keep them quietly in the background as they tend to get over-excited. I actually had a child pick up a puppy when my back was turned. The puppy wriggled and fell from the child's arms. Luckily the puppy was all right, but the child was very distressed.

It is rare to be allowed to pick a puppy at this age as the breeder will probably not have made his final decision, but you could at least see the litter and possibly express a preference.

If you are allowed to choose a puppy on your first visit the old saying of 'let the puppy choose you' is not a bad one. Provided the litter all look healthy and active, the chances are that if you are looking for a pet, whichever one you choose will be just fine. After all, that puppy has every chance of growing up in the way you mould him just like a child would (we hope). The puppies should all have shiny healthy coats, clear bright eyes, which should not be running or wet (*see* Chapter 11), and cold wet noses. They should be well covered but not grossly fat, and not pot-bellied as this can be a sign of worms. If you are looking for a show prospect look carefully at coats. Often while puppies are still in the nest you can get a clue as to the type of adult coat to expect: if looking for liver, go for a good dark shade. Try to avoid a slightly wavy coat, which will often show on the young puppy just behind the head and sometimes continuing down the neck and back. This will nearly always develop into a thick, wavy, hard-to-manage adult coat. Also be sure that the nose has good pigmentation. A little pink still showing will probably fill in, but if there is too much, you will finish up with an adult dog with a partially pigmented ('butterfly') nose, which is a fault in the show ring. Look at eye colour: the darker the blue, the better the chance of finishing up with a good dark hazel eye. Although these are only the puppy's first teeth he should still have a correct bite (*see* Chapter 2), and two testicles should be descending into the scrotum by the time the male puppy is six to eight weeks old, be they only about the size of peas. It can sometimes take longer for the testicles to drop, but if you are choosing a show puppy it is important that he is entire and the risk that they may not drop should not be taken.

The puppies should all come forward to meet you with wagging tails. If one hangs back just a little do not dismiss him immediately – he may only just have woken up, or may simply be a bit of a thinker. Do, however, be wary of a puppy or puppies who are reluctant to come to you at all or who seem nervous of sudden noise. Remember this is the environment they are used to and so this is where they should be at their most confident. Having said that, you will sometimes find that one puppy is being bullied by his siblings, and will come out of himself when removed from them or when they have gone.

If there are only one or two puppies left when you are offered the chance to look at a litter, do not think that these are necessarily the worst and so not worth considering. Often the opposite is true and the breeder has in fact kept back the best until last, with the thought that if they do not sell to good pet homes then they are the most likely to go on to show or work.

It may be that, after going through all of this, the breeder decides that you are not the right person to own one of his dogs, or that the environment in which you wish to keep the dog is not right. Whatever his reasoning, it should be respected, as hard as that may be.

The Paperwork

Assuming all has gone well and you have chosen your new puppy, you will want to see the pedigree before making your final decision (reading the pedigree is explained in Chapter 9). By the time the puppy is ready to go, his registration papers should be back from the Kennel Club. These papers may have been endorsed by the breeder and if this is the case it is up to the breeder to make you aware of these endorsements and what they mean. The possible endorsements are: (a) Not eligible for entry at shows, field trials or working trials held under Kennel Club regulations; (b) Progeny not eligible for registration; (c) Not eligible for the issue of an export pedigree; or (d) Name unchangeable. These endorsements, if applied for, are printed on the front of the registration certificate and so are easy to see. They can be removed by the breeder at any time if the breeder applies in writing to the Kennel Club.

With the Kennel Club registration papers comes six weeks' free insurance cover, valid from the moment you apply for change of ownership. This will all be explained to you in detail by the breeder.

It may be that your new puppy is over eight weeks old and has been vaccinated, in which case you will require the vaccination certificate signed by the veterinary surgeon, and information about the second vaccination.

You should receive a diet sheet giving full instructions on all that the puppy will have to eat and drink from the time of leaving the breeder through to adulthood, listing quantities as well as products used. This should also include details of previous worming and advice on a future worming programme.

Do remember that even the most reputable breeders can only do their best, and that there can be no guarantees.

4

Caring for your Puppy

Before taking your puppy home be sure that you are quite ready for him. Do remember that it is very important to start as you mean to go on, and that the time you spend with your puppy in these formative months will pay dividends in the long run.

Sleeping Quarters

Is your puppy to sleep indoors or outside? Wherever it is, a warm comfortable bed should have been prepared, and do remember that this is where he must sleep. It is quite likely that he may whine or even howl on the first night or two, and it is most important that you leave him where he is, as hard as that may be. It is rather like having a new baby in the house, and the old adage of 'provided he is well fed and comfortable leave him alone' seems to apply to both. He has to learn that this is now his home and that sleeping alone is to become the norm. Unless you plan to let him spend the rest of his days sleeping on your bed then do start as you mean to go on, as difficult as that may seem at the time.

If he is to sleep out in a kennel, make sure that it is warm and draught free. His bed should be raised off the ground a little to bring it above the draughts that may come under the door.

Many types of bedding are available. Personally, I still like to use wheat straw for outdoor bedding as the dogs can make a nest for themselves in it. If you do choose this for your puppy, be sure to settle it down before putting the puppy in or he may find himself buried in it. There are different types of shredded paper available now for bedding, but when I tried using some I found that puppies tended to get tangled up in it, and were also inclined to drag it out of the bed and all around the kennel. Probably the best type of paper, that does not cause these problems is shredded newspaper, but then this tends to make the white parts of your dog a little discoloured. Old blankets are useful for bedding but again, I have found that puppies tend to drag them out of the bed and finish up lying on nothing. You can also buy a type of very good, hard-backed fleecy bedding for dogs, but I have found that although this tends to stay in place quite well when new, once it has been washed a few times and has softened, then this also gets dragged out of the bed.

If your puppy is to sleep indoors, then a warm, draught-free position for his bed is best. Personally, I feel that the best type of bed is an old cardboard box, with a piece cut out of the front for puppy to get in and out through. There will be plenty of time for a smart dog bed once the chewing stage is over. Bedding to be used in the house is obviously another consideration, and an old blanket or piece of fleecy bed will do nicely and will also be easy to wash.

Do remember that if your puppy has come from a kennel he may find the house a little warm at first. Likewise, if it is winter and he has come from a house and is to be housed in a kennel, it will need heating in a safe way, with no wires about for him to chew.

Feeding Bowls and Toys

Both indoors and outside, a few toys will help to keep him amused whilst he is alone, which inevitably he will be at times. Do think carefully when buying him things to play with. Many of the toys available for pets are far too easy to chew up and eat, so try to buy the indestructible type. His water and feed bowls might also become 'toys', therefore the stainless steel type are probably the best buy, being easy to wash and difficult to chew! For a kennelled dog, I would advise obtaining a holder for the water bowl, that can be attached to the wall or door and that will help to prevent water being spilt all over the kennel. Whilst you are in the pet shop buying your equipment, another useful purchase would be a spray of 'bitter apple'. This is a harmless liquid which can be sprayed on to things that you particularly do not want chewing, and it tastes horrid.

Feeding

As already mentioned, your puppy should have his own diet sheet, which you will have seen prior to bringing him home in order for

A water bowl correctly secured and away from shavings on the floor.

This puppy eats happily from a bowl designed to keep the ears out of the food.

you to buy his food ready for his arrival. If you do not wish to continue to feed him in the way that the breeder has done so far, that is up to you, but it is advisable to start him off on what he is used to. Many breeders will give you a 'starter kit' with your puppy, which makes life easier. Please do be advised to continue with his usual diet, at least for the first couple of weeks, unless advised otherwise by your veterinary surgeon. There will already be enough different things for your puppy to have to get used to and he is most likely to continue to eat well, and not have an upset tummy, if his diet is stable.

He may not eat as much as you would expect, or as much as is on his diet sheet at first. This is quite normal. Do not be tempted to try to make him eat by offering him little delicacies. Generally speaking, loss of appetite will just be a result of change of environment, and he will eat when he is hungry.

A breeder will normally suggest that you collect your puppy first thing in the morning in order to give him the full day to settle. In addition, I usually send mine off with an empty stomach to lessen the likelihood of them being sick in the car, and so that on arrival at their new home they are hungry. English Springers have a very good appetite as a general rule, but do not worry if your puppy does not seem to want to eat for the first twenty-four hours. He will not come to any harm for a day without food, and the chances are that the next day he will wake up hungry.

A great variety of excellent food products are available for rearing puppies, and if you are not happy with the diet provided by your puppy's breeder, please do be sure only to wean him over to something different gradually. If he looks well, is happy, healthy, and gaining weight nicely I would advise you to stick with what he is on. If he is not thriving, seek veterinary advice to eliminate other causes before changing his diet.

There are many excellent complete foods now on the market, both moist and dry. My vet persuaded me off the traditional ways of rearing puppies and onto the complete dry system, and I have to admit that, although I took some convincing, I would not go back to the other system, which involved preparing fresh foods. I would not say that the puppies are being reared any better than on the traditional system, but the way I feed now is much easier, cleaner and more economical. By the time my puppies leave home they are on four meals a day, two of tinned puppy meat mixed with dry expanded puppy biscuit, and two of soaked dry food. By feeding them this way they are getting all of the necessary vitamins and minerals they require, and their future owners can choose whether they are going to continue as they have been fed, or change on to a dry food diet or a meat diet, with little disruption to the puppies' digestive systems.

My only slight criticism of the dry foods is that, in my experience, the manufacturers' instructions tend to advise rather too much food for an English Springer. You will probably find that if you feed the quantities they recommend, your puppy may get a little overweight.

It is also worth noting that with the complete foods, either dry or moist, it is not necessary to give your puppy anything to drink other than water, which does seem strange, as we all tend to expect to give babies milk, but milk is not necessary and would in fact spoil the balance of feed.

If you feel strongly that you want to feed your puppy on the traditional or 'old fashioned' type of food, then you will need to make the transition very carefully, and you will need to buy some good wholemeal puppy biscuit, which will need soaking, some good quality pet mince and/or minced green tripe, a good calcium and phosphorus supplement, a general vitamin supplement, which must include Vitamin D to aid absorption of the calcium, and some dried puppy milk. The milk will need mixing and must be fed according to the instructions on the wrapping. The mince and/or tripe can be fed raw, but I would advise cooking it, and it should then be mixed with the soaked meal and topped with a little calcium and vitamin supplement according to manufacturers' recommendations.

It is not necessary to add these extras to the complete foods as they are already included, and if you do add them you will upset the balance that has been carefully achieved by the manufacturer, and will in fact do more harm than good.

It is worth remembering that if you allow your puppy to become a fussy feeder now, the chances are that he will always be fussy. It is a good idea to give him ten minutes to eat his food up, and any that he may have left after that time should be taken away. This will normally result in the puppy realising that food is not on offer constantly and he should be eating up well within a few days. Do not worry if he is not eating all of his food at first though, as long as he is well. You will doubtless be taking him to your veterinary surgeon within a few days of bringing him home for a check-over and his vaccinations, and he will advise you further about the correct weight for your puppy. Do remember it is as bad for growing puppies to be too fat as it is for them to be too thin, as carrying too much weight puts strain on developing bones and ligaments.

Upset Stomach

Sometimes the change of environment, and even different water, can upset a puppy's stomach even if his food has not been changed. I find that homeopathy has its uses in the canine world, and one of the most effective remedies is Arsen Alb or, to give it its full name, Asenicum Album (White Arsenic). I use it at the potency of 30c and it can easily be bought at any health shop and many chemists. I have found Arsen Alb excellent for upset stomachs in dogs and simply crush a tablet between two clean spoons, and then dribble a little of the powder onto the puppy's tongue. As with all homeopathic remedies, the palate should be clean when the remedy is administered and food should be withheld for at least twenty minutes afterwards. I would dose in this way every half an hour for four doses, and then three times per day. If the puppy's stomach had not settled within 24 hours then I would seek veterinary advice. It could be that the puppy had eaten something such as a stone, and the resultant diarrhoea can be very debilitating, especially in the young. With an older dog withholding food will often help settle an upset stomach, but this is not advisable with a puppy.

Vaccinations

Puppies can have their first vaccination from eight weeks of age onwards and the second part of the two-vaccination course four weeks later. The vaccinations are to protect the puppy from distemper (hardpad), leptospirosis, hepatitis and parvovirus, and a booster should be given annually to ensure continued protection.

It is advisable not to allow your puppy to mix with other dogs until one week after his first injection, if vaccinated at 8 weeks, although he will have some maternal immunity.

Your veterinary surgeon will give you a vaccination certificate showing your puppy's details and a record of the vaccinations given. Should you wish to put your puppy in boarding kennels at any time, or take him to training classes, you will be required to show this certificate so do be sure to keep it somewhere safe.

Kennel Club Registration Certificate

The other certificate you will have with your puppy is the Kennel Club registration certificate (as mentioned in Chapter 3). Do remember to fill this in and post it off to the Kennel Club with the relevant fee, as this not only transfers the puppy into your name but also gives you six weeks' free insurance cover for your puppy.

Teething

By the time you take your puppy home from his breeder he should have all of his first teeth. At about twelve weeks these will start to come loose, and gradually, over a period of approximately six weeks, they will fall out and be replaced by adult teeth. The time it takes for a puppy to change his teeth does seem to vary from puppy to puppy, even within a litter, and should not cause any problem. It is a good idea to keep an eye on your puppy's mouth during this time as occasionally a new tooth may try to force its way through before the baby tooth has gone. It may then be necessary to take a quick trip to the vet's and have the first tooth removed to allow the second tooth to grow through in the correct place.

As with children, the first teeth to change will be the two centre incisors, and the last teeth to come through will be the premolars and molars; these are the ones which just might cause sufficient discomfort to put your puppy off his food, particularly if he is being fed dry food. It just may be necessary to soak his food for a while whilst these teeth come through.

In my opinion the teeth most likely to cause problems when they are changing are the canines. It is often the case with these teeth that the first tooth is still firmly in place and the second tooth can be seen coming through alongside it. Sometimes the second tooth will come through and appear to be growing in such a way that it will stick in to the roof of the mouth rather than fit neatly round the edge as it should. In all cases without exception where I have seen this happen, the tooth has finished up in the correct position in the mouth, but obviously if you are worried and consider your puppy to be in pain then seek veterinary advice.

Worming

During these first few weeks of life in his new home your puppy will need worming more regularly than he will in later life. He will have been wormed several times by his breeder before coming to you. Hopefully, his breeder will have given you details of dates and products used in previous wormings, and it is advisable to take these with you to your veterinary surgeon on your first visit so that he can then advise on a continued worming programme. The modern wormers are very effective. It is unusual actually to see worms in a puppy's faeces, but this does not mean that the puppy is free from worms, and the only effective way to check for worm presence is for a veterinary surgeon to run a test. Provided your puppy is healthy and growing well, however, this should not be necessary.

Advances in modern science have meant that wormers, like dog foods, have progressed greatly in recent years, and I do feel that it is best to use a product supplied by your vet as they keep right up to date with progress.

House-training

Probably the most stressful aspect of introducing a new puppy to the home, both for you and the puppy, is house-training. The answer is to be diligent, and to start as soon as the puppy arrives home. Once he thinks it is acceptable to mess in the house then it will be more difficult to break him of the habit. The younger the puppy, the more often he will need to relieve himself. If you observe him carefully it is easy to see the warning signs: he will look for the right place, sniffing the floor and walking round in small circles. This is the moment to take him gently outside to the area that you have decided it is acceptable to him to use. Having disturbed his train of thought you will have to be patient and wait while he finds what he considers to be the right spot. As soon as he has done what is necessary praise him. Do be sure to wait until he has finished though, otherwise you may get the rest when back in the house!

Obviously this waiting about outside is more acceptable for both you and your puppy on a warm summer's day than in the depths of winter, so do be sure that if it is cold and wet your puppy is not getting chilled by standing outside for too long. English Springers are quite tough, but the difference between a centrally heated house and a chilly February day can be rather extreme. Summer is an easier time than winter to house-train puppies, with the longer days and tendency to have the doors open to the garden, but this advantage of having a summer puppy is sometimes outweighed by the fact that you may want to go away on a summer holiday and it is not easy, or very kind, to leave a young puppy in a strange environment.

Your puppy will need to be taken outside to his allotted area as soon as he wakes up in the morning, after any nap he has during the day, after every meal and at any other time he shows signs of needing to go. As he gets older the need to go so often will lessen, so do not despair if at first it seems like an awful lot of standing about outside.

He will not be able to go through the whole night without relieving himself, even allowing for the fact that you will take him out last thing. It is therefore a good idea to surround his bed with newspapers which, as he gets used to using them, can gradually be

Garden exploration can be tremendous fun.

moved towards the door so that eventually it becomes natural for him to go to the door to do his business. A natural progression from this, when the door is open, will be to go outside.

Always taking him to the same area outside should teach him that this is the place you would like him to use, which means that you only have one small area of the garden to clean up. Most good pet shops now sell various types of bins for the disposal of faeces and it is best for you to choose whichever suits your lifestyle. At first it will be easier to carry your puppy out to do his business, but as soon as he will follow you let him walk as this will help him get the idea of going out to his allotted spot when he feels inclined. Accidents are bound to happen and if you see one happening then do scold him, just as you would praise him for going outside, but remember that a puppy's memory is very short, so it is no good scolding him for something he did when you were not there: merely clear it up and remove any smell to discourage him from going there again.

In the unfortunate event of the puppy making a stain on the best rug, stain removers are also available from good pet shops, and are said to be very effective.

Socializing

I am a great believer in letting your puppy learn about life as young as is sensible. The noises about the house are a good start for a young puppy: the washing machine, the vacuum cleaner and the television are all things to experience, things that the kennelled dog will miss out on. Therefore it is probably more important to allow the kennelled dog access to the big, wide world. Little visits into the house would also be beneficial to start with.

Once puppy's vaccinations are effective then little trips out, even if only in your arms to visit the neighbours, do help to get him used to the idea that there is a big world out there beyond the boundaries of house and kennel and will help to avoid a shy or over-cautious dog later in life.

The Car

As soon as he is safely vaccinated, short trips in the car, perhaps to the shops or to fetch the children from school, are a good idea. Little and often in the car from an early age will pay dividends later on in helping to avoid travel sickness. If you have a persistently bad traveller, then I strongly believe that prevention is better than cure: pet shops and vets sell travel pills for dogs. I use travel pills made for humans, which are available at chemist shops. If I find that giving one two hours before the journey does not help, then I give one the night before and that will normally work for the most difficult traveller.

I feel that the first introduction to the car is most important. Provided your new purchase is small enough I firmly believe that the best place for your puppy to travel until he is confident is on someone's lap, on some old towels, preferably in the front of the car. Once he is happy and confident in the car he can then be taught to travel in the rear, preferably in a cage or behind a dog guard. This is far safer for you and him than having him gambolling around the car while you are trying to drive. I have even heard of a case where a car owner's insurance company would not pay out on an insurance claim after an accident because there was no guard in the car, even though the dog was in no way responsible for the accident.

Insurance

Your puppy will have come to you with his six weeks of free insurance cover from the Kennel Club, and before that runs out it is worth considering whether or not you wish to extend this, or to insure with another company, or simply not to insure.

In my opinion the most important part of the insurance is the third party liability cover, which you may find included on your household policy. You may or may not consider the health cover to be financially viable.

Lead-Training

By the time your puppy is clear of his injections (at approximately three months old), you can start some gentle lead-training. First let him get used to wearing a soft collar: a cat collar is not a bad idea if it fits and if you do not mind buying something that you know you will only use for a very short time. Once your puppy has been wearing this for short periods, probably only five minutes at a time to start with for about one week, try attaching a lead and very gently let him get the idea that he cannot run off where he chooses when the lead is on. Again, the lead you use now will not be his grown-up lead, as that would be too heavy for his little neck.

It may be best when first using the lead to stand still and just let the puppy learn that he has to respect your wishes and stand still with you. Do remember to give him lots of praise when he does well, and try not to frighten him. All lessons at this early age should only last for five or ten minutes. Little and often is far better than boring him silly. After he has accepted the collar and lead happily, encourage him to walk with you. Just a few steps at a time at first and then give lots of praise. Do try to avoid dragging him along by his neck, or he will soon associate the collar and lead with unpleasant experiences and be reluctant to have them on.

During the third and fourth months of your puppy's life, lead-training for ten minutes a day, three or four days a week will be plenty. He will become bored with more, and even more importantly, if he has too much enforced exercise at this tender age when his bones, muscles and ligaments are still developing, you could do him untold damage. Playing for short periods in the garden, he will decide when he has had enough and just flop where he is and have a rest, or take himself off to bed. Just like young children, young dogs should not be asked to do too much, mentally or physically, in these early months. Remember the ratio of one year in human terms to seven years in dogs'; you would not expect a three-and-a-half-year-old child to go for a five-mile hike, and yet it is amazing how many people expect their six-month-old puppy to.

Children

If there are children in the home with your new puppy it is important that they understand the ground rules regarding him. It is vital that they do not treat the puppy as a toy, and that they respect his privacy and understand that he needs to have a routine and abide by the rules of the house just as they do.

If you have very young children, do remember that they might not understand that it is wrong, and very painful for the puppy, if they grab at his ears, legs and tail, etc. In the same way, the puppy will not understand that it is wrong to bite the children in play.

98

Older children should be taught that the puppy needs continuity in his training, and they must learn to mirror you in their treatment of him.

English Springers make wonderful friends for children, and a little patience and understanding at this age will be well worthwhile.

Commands

All commands must be easy for the puppy to understand. The words he will probably hear most are his name and 'No'. Do remember that he is young and needs praise as well as chastisement. Repetition is the best way for him to learn, provided he is not allowed to get bored.

Keep commands simple. It is no good having a conversation with him and expecting him to understand. His name (to catch his attention) and one-word commands are by far the best, not forgetting the praise when he does right. The words you will use the most are 'Come', 'Sit', 'No', 'Fetch', 'Stay' and, the exception to the one-word rule, 'Good boy'.

Very Basic Obedience

In the first three months of your puppy's life there will be a great deal of new experiences for him, and obedience training as such will be non-existent. Day-to-day happenings, however, will start to form the basis of his training. From the start it is expected that your puppy will come happily to you when you call him, and do remember always to praise him for doing so.

If, as he grows up, he becomes wilful and starts to ignore you or run away when called, I have found that the best way to get a wilful puppy back is to run and hide from him. You may feel rather foolish, but in the confines of your own home there will be no one to see you and no danger of puppy getting lost. It is amazing how quickly they come looking for you. As soon as he does give him lots of praise. I would be reluctant at this age to resort to giving him titbits, although these are useful in later training.

If you want your Springer to retrieve later in life it is never too soon to start, but if you have children this is not an exercise for them to practise, as it must not become a rough game. Just four or five

A puppy performing a simple retrieve with a glove, showing that the natural instinct is already there.

short retrieves with something soft such as an old sock or glove is plenty to start with, and remember to give lots of praise. Do not be too formal about it; let puppy enjoy what he is doing. There will be plenty of time to teach him to wait before he is allowed to fetch his article when he gets to six or seven months of age.

He can start to be taught very gently to sit on command, and maybe to wait for his food to be put down, his collar to be put on or the door to be opened. Depending on your dog's future career it may be that you do not want him to sit. If he is hopefully going to be a show dog then you would really prefer him to stand, and many people would advise training in that from the start. I am not so sure. It is very difficult to get a young puppy to stand still, whereas the very act of sitting immobilizes him, and being immobilized can be very useful, if only for a split second, as it may give you the opportunity to catch his collar or scruff of the neck in a potentially dangerous situation.

I find that it is quite possible to teach the sit and, once that is firmly fixed in his mind, then to teach the stand. Having said that, if you are hoping to show your puppy I do believe that it is useful to teach him to stand still on a table while supported by your hands from a very early age. This gives him the feel of how you want him

100

to stand, and somehow if dogs have practised this from an early age they seem to find it easier to balance themselves in the stand.

It should be easy at this early age to put your puppy gently in to the sit position, whilst using the command 'Sit', if you keep his head up and put a little pressure on his quarters. With whatever exercise you are practising, little and often and lots of praise is always the best way. It may be that 'Sit' is not the command you wish to use: the word does not matter, as long as that same word is used by the whole of the family. If it has been decided that your dog will never be fed from the table, then he must be shown where it is acceptable for him to sit whilst the family is eating and *no one* should *ever* feed him from the table. Likewise, if it is decided that he should never go upstairs or sit on the furniture, the same applies: *everyone* must enforce that decision.

Training Classes

Most training classes now take puppies from about four months of age, in what is more of a social event than training and rather like the doggy version of nursery. I would not think that this was really necessary for a puppy destined for field trials, but it is definitely useful for pet and show puppies.

Your vet's surgery, pet shops and library should have details of local dog training clubs.

Early Grooming

If simple grooming is introduced from the start your puppy will learn to sit still and enjoy the attention, and it may well save many a wrestling match when he gets older.

The tips of his ears will probably need washing after he has had any wet food. He should learn to be brushed: at this age a soft brush is ideal just to let him get the feel of it without risk of it hurting or pulling on his coat. He also needs to have his toe-nails trimmed regularly. If he has white nails it is quite easy to see how far to trim them back, as the quick and blood supply show, but with a black nail it is far more difficult. Although it is quite unpleasant for both you and your puppy if you do draw blood, do not worry: it will soon stop and you will know to take a little less off next time.

He will not have much feather yet, but a little comb through what he does have will get him used to the idea, as will a little trim round the shape of the foot with the straight scissors. (Trimming is described more fully in Chapter 7.)

Summary

What must be remembered through all of this is that he is a dog, and is not to be confused with a human. Dogs live in a very different way to us. In the wild they respect a very strict pecking order. It is essential that you come at the top of his order, and that whilst your dog is a part of your family he understands that in that order he comes below all humans, children included. The English Springer is a delightful breed and there is no reason that there should ever be a temperament problem, but if there is one, the reason is bound to be that the dog has lost sight of that pecking order.

5

Adolescent and Adult Management

As the months pass, you and your Springer will be developing a bond. You will get to know each other's ways, and will learn how far you can push each other. I shall continue through this chapter in general terms on management and training of your dog, starting from about six months of age, although it should be remembered that different dogs progress at different speeds. Chapter 6 contains more specialist training advice.

Exercise and Training

As your Springer matures in body and mind, so his exercise and training can increase, but only a little at a time. It is still important not to overdo it from a structural point of view, and not to get him bored and resentful. By now he will have grown out of his puppy collar and you will need to get him a nice leather collar that is to be his, hopefully, for life, unless it gets chewed up, of course!

You may not wish to walk him on a collar and lead any more, but may prefer the extra control given by a check-chain. If so, it is important that this is fitted correctly. The chain should be just long enough to fit comfortably over your dog's head, with approximately three inches of chain spare when it is pulled tight on the neck. Presuming that you are walking with your dog on your left hand side (which is normal) the chain should be put on with the ring lying nearest to your left leg, and with the part of the chain that joins to the lead coming over the back of the neck, through the ring and pulling uphill away from your left leg. This way, when you relax the lead the chain will go slack.

If you are planning to show your Springer, remember that the constant use of a check-chain, or leaving a collar on permanently, will damage the hair round his neck and be detrimental to his appearance in the ring. There are other types of slip-leads that will afford you more control than an ordinary collar, and it is a matter of personal choice which you use. If you are going to training classes you will probably be advised there.

Your Springer can now be building up his enforced exercise to twenty minutes per day. If you are training him every day, take the training time out of his enforced exercise time. Do not bore him with too much training at this age, and do not overdo the exercise, as it can still do untold damage to young bones and ligaments. It is better to give him less than twenty minutes, rather than more.

At this age it is important that, like a small child's, his brain is being stimulated, and that he is given small challenges. By this I do not mean that he should be training for Obedience Champion of the Year, but merely that his everyday routine should include things to keep him amused, things like meeting cattle or sheep for the first time, learning to carry your glove a short distance, or meeting next door's cat – and not chasing it; generally learning to be part of the society in which he is living.

Lead-training should be going on nicely with your dog walking calmly to heel on your left-hand side. If he is a little boisterous and inclined to pull, then a sharp jerk on the lead, combined with the command 'Heel', should bring him back to where you want him. As soon as he has responded satisfactorily, remember to praise him. If you are using a slip-lead or check-chain, which would be advisable with a dog inclined to pull, as you give a sharp jerk on the lead it will tighten and become uncomfortable on your dog's neck. As soon as you release the pressure, so it will slacken off (if fitted correctly), and hopefully the dog will soon learn to associate pulling with that jerk and the unpleasant pressure, and walking nicely to heel with praise.

Recall

During this time the recall exercise can be continued with your dog learning to come whenever called, from whatever he may be doing about the house and garden, and starting to learn to sit nicely in front of you on returning. Do remember the instant praise. If the sit is a little slow do not worry: the most important thing at this age is that he is coming. If you chastise him for not sitting he will think

'Well, I came and I'm getting told off. I will not bother to come next time.' The sit is a useful finish to the exercise, particularly if your dog has filthy feet and is inclined to jump up when he is called, but the most important thing is that he comes.

Do not be tempted to formalize the recall by making your dog wait before coming at this stage in his training. It is better to get the stay exercise consolidated before confusing him with 'Wait'.

Once the stay exercise is firmly fixed in his mind, and I do mean *firmly*, then the command 'Wait' can be introduced. By using two different words for what, at first impression, would seem to be the same exercise, you will make it easier for your dog to understand that although he has to stay initially, on command he is then allowed to move. With the 'Stay' command he does not move until the exercise is completed, and the handler returned to his side.

Do remember through all of these exercises that praise is all-important. Your dog will respond much better to training if he knows that he is going to get lots of fuss when he does well. The tone of your voice is as important as what you say, and the very act of telling him that he is good and has done well changes the tone of your voice from command to praise.

To carry out the more formal recall, put your dog in the sit position and give him the command 'Wait'. Back away from him, re-enforcing the command if you think he is going to move, and holding up the palm of your hand to face him, as if to push him back. Do not go too far from him initially and do be sure not to call him in until you are ready to. It is very tempting to see that he is about to move and so call him.

Once you are happy that he understands the command 'Wait', and that he is waiting to be recalled happily and coming straight to you on request, then you can be more particular about him sitting nicely in front of you. Ideally, he should sit facing you, directly in front of your legs, but as we are not aiming at competitive obedience, provided he sits still in front of you with his attention focused on you, that seems quite adequate to my mind.

Once this is firmly established in his mind and to your satisfaction, to finish off the exercise correctly you will bring him to heel. The idea of this is that sitting at heel on your left-hand side is a very convenient position for you either to slip on his lead or to walk on with him by your side.

To teach him to come to heel it is easier initially to slip the lead on first. This part of the exercise need not be taught at the end of

105

With the handler holding the lead in the right hand, the dog is guided round to heel following the right leg back.

As the dog passes behind the handler the lead is changed from right hand to left hand and the dog is encouraged to follow the left leg forward.

The dog follows the left leg forward to the sit position, helped by the lead in the left hand if necessary.

the recall to start with, but can be made into a separate exercise that can even be practised indoors when you have five minutes to spare. Start with your dog sitting in front facing you with his lead on. Holding the lead in your right hand, step back on your right leg, simultaneously giving the command 'Heel' and, if necessary, giving the lead a small jerk before passing it behind your back in to your left hand. As your right leg moves forward out of the way, your left hand will guide your dog to your left-hand side and into the sit position. Give him lots of praise in the sit position.

That might sound complicated but it is not really, and it is amazing how quickly your dog will learn that part of the exercise.

The Stay

As you are progressing through these early months your puppy will be learning to stay, in various situations, so this exercise just becomes part of life. Sitting and waiting for his food or to have his collar put on are both short stay exercises, therefore it should not be difficult to continue this into a more formal training.

Start with short sit or down stays, whichever you feel that your dog is most likely to stay still in. On first consideration you would imagine that the down stay would be the easier of the two, but this is not necessarily so as with the down stay the dog feels further away from your hands, the most usual form of contact, and may be tempted to sit up when you return to him.

Whichever position you choose, put your dog in that position and give the command 'Stay', then, as with the recall, back away from the dog, re-enforcing the command if you consider it necessary with your hand held up, palm facing him. When you stop do not stand straight on to him, as you would in a recall, but stand slightly sideways-on. Start by only standing still for a few seconds, then return to his side. Always praise him in the same position you left him in, then let him move, and reposition him before starting again. As he gets steadier you can progress to walking round him in a small circle, re-enforcing the command 'Stay' at any sign of him getting up and, again giving lots of praise before he is allowed to move.

As you progress with this exercise your dog will get steadier and

The Stay, showing the hand held up to reinforce the command.

steadier and he will learn to stay in the stand, sit and down positions. Yet again, this can be useful in everyday life. I can think of one instance, when we were living in a built-up area, when one of my dogs nipped across the road after a cat when I was not looking (not thorough-enough cat training), and only the fact that I could quickly command the dog to stay where he was saved him from being run over on his way back across the road.

The Law and Your Dog

By law, any dog in a public place must wear a collar with a name tag on it. Name tags can usually be bought and engraved at cobblers' shops.

It is also against the law for your dog to foul in a public place. Whenever you are out walking with your dog you should have a supply of plastic bags in your pocket, coloured if you do not like to see what you are doing, to clear up any mess that he may make. It is very simple to put your hand inside the bag, rather like putting on a glove, pick up the mess, turn the bag inside out, and tie the top. This way the mess can be hygienically disposed of in the nearest rubbish bin, or taken home.

Dogs should always be kept on leads when walking public footpaths where there are cattle or sheep in the field.

Feeding

I shall keep this as brief and as straightforward as possible, because the feeding of a healthy Springer should not produce any problems and, as I have said before, the modern dog foods are so well balanced that all the hard work has been taken out of the job for you. Having said that, it is important to keep your dog at the correct weight and growing at the correct rate. I have heard it said that if you keep a growing Springer short of protein you can curb his growth, and that if you let a growing Springer gallop about too much he will grow tall and leggy. I am sure that there is no scientific proof to substantiate these theories, but that does not necessarily mean that there is no truth in them.

Provided you keep your Springer on the correct product for his age group and feed at or just below the manufacturer's recommended quantities, whilst keeping his exercise to a sensible level to allow bones, ligaments and muscles to develop, I do not feel that you should have any problems.

Obviously, if the breeder of your puppy has provided you with a diet sheet through to adulthood, and has been insistent that this is the best possible way to feed him, then, provided he is looking well, stick with the diet sheet.

The exceptions to this are when your dog does not appear to be behaving or looking right on what you are feeding him. Some dogs become excitable on high-protein food, others may get skin irritation, and others loose faeces. Should this be the case with your dog, his food will need to be changed by a process of elimination to see what is causing the problem and to find how best to rectify it. Some dogs benefit from a wheat-free diet and will do well on a rice-based complete food. Others may need a higher fat level, less protein or more starch. Whatever the case remember that if your dog is still growing it may be necessary to add extra vitamins and/or minerals if you change the balance of the correct food for his age group, so do try to change the food within the manufacturer's recommendations for his age.

It is important to maintain the level of calories in a growing dog's diet because at this stage he requires two to three times more calories per unit of bodyweight than an adult dog. It should also be remembered that an adult working dog will use more energy than a pet dog or show dog and will therefore require a diet with a higher fat content to provide energy density. The various manufacturers of dog foods have spent a great deal of money on research into these requirements and there is now a very comprehensive range of products on the market to suit all needs.

If you have problems choosing the best diet for your dog, the bigger manufacturers have a very helpful team of specialists who are only too happy to offer advice and give out samples.

At the other end of the scale, do remember that as puppies have different requirements to young dogs, so old dogs have different requirements to young dogs and, as they take less exercise with the advancing years, their bodily functions will slow down and their food should be adjusted accordingly. Old dogs will need lower levels of fat and protein than active young dogs, and it is quite a good idea to cut their meals in half and feed twice daily to help digestion.

Housing

If your English Springer is to be your only dog and purely a family pet, the likelihood is that he will live in the house as an extension of the family. Even so, rules must be laid down for the benefit of both the family and the dog. As mentioned earlier it must be decided how far through the house the dog's territory will go: is he allowed everywhere, including on the bed? This is not really a good idea as it is putting the dog on equal footing with you, apart from the fact that a wet, smelly Springer is not a very suitable bedmate. If you really do feel very strongly that you want the dog in the bedroom with you, give him his own bed on the floor and make it very clear from the start that this is where he is to sleep.

The limits of where he is allowed can be whatever you choose to make them, as long as it is agreed by all of the family and made clear to the dog from the start.

Once he is through the chewing stage there are several different types of bed that you can consider for him. Personally, I like the

Kennel mates but not litter mates.

111

moulded plastic type as they are easy to keep clean and protect the dog from any draughts, and the bedding you use in them, be it old blankets or a fleecy bed, can easily be washed. I find that a bean bag or quilt large enough for a Springer tends not to fit in my washing machine, and that although most have removable covers the inside really needs washing as well.

If you want your dog to be kennelled for all or part of the day then a sturdy, draught-free kennel should be provided, preferably with an outdoor run. I would say that a building measuring 4ft (1.2m) by 5ft 6in (1.65m) would be suitable, with a raised bed across the back coming forward 2ft 6in (75cm). The bed should have an 18in (45cm)-high front on it to allow for a good, deep wheat-straw bed. This high front would only be suitable for adult dogs and would be too high for puppies.

The door should have a small access hole in it which can be closed when necessary. Ideally, the outdoor run should measure the same size, or be a little larger than the kennel and should have a roof to keep off the worst of the rain and sun.

This size of building would house one or two Springers provided they were also given adequate exercise.

If you are planning to start your own small kennel then you will obviously need more kennel space, dependent on numbers of dogs. Converted stables make good indoor kennels with each average-sized stable splitting well into two indoor kennels.

An interesting point to remember is that if your kennelled dog's bed is too large you may find that he will mess in it, whereas he will rarely mess on the spot where he is going to sleep.

If building kennels from scratch you should consider how near to the house you want them: too near and you may get a noise nuisance, too far and it is a long way to walk to control any noise and oversee security.

I always bring my bitches into the house to whelp, but if you are planning to whelp them outside then you must consider how far it will seem in the middle of the night, when distance always seems much greater.

In an ideal world you will have lights, including heat lamps, in your kennels, power points and hot and cold water. Remember that all of these services must be safely protected from the dogs. A good-quality fire extinguisher should also be mounted at a readily accessible point in the kennels.

The best way, in my opinion, to keep your kennels smelling sweet

Mrs Wendy Adam's Sh.Ch. Wenark Justin Step pictured at twelve years of age. 'William' is living proof of the longevity of the English Springer (see Appendix II for pedigree).

is to use shavings for the floor. A light sprinkling is not too expensive, soaks up the urine, and seems to take away the worst of the smell of the faeces. This can be swept up daily and burnt in an incinerator. The kennels should be washed out with a suitable kennel disinfectant once weekly and the bedding burnt, the beds sprayed with a good insecticidal spray, and fresh bedding put in. Leave the kennel for half an hour after this has been done before putting the dogs back in.

If you move into the breeder category you will need to get a breeder's licence (*see* Chapter 9), and to comply with the requirements of your local council. It may therefore be sensible to check with the council what these requirements are before starting your building or conversion.

6

Training

The English Springer could do anything, I'm sure, that he cared to put his mind to; however, he is historically better suited to some things than others and these are the things on which I shall concentrate.

Obedience

Springers have been successful in obedience competitions, some even getting to the top-class events; however; the requirement for total precision in this field does tend to mean that the Border Collie is generally recognized as the best dog for the job. It is useful, though, to take your dog to obedience training classes to socialize him and teach him how to be an acceptable member of society. If you do want to have a go at competitive obedience the best way to progress from the basic training described in Chapter 5 is to join your local training club. There is bound to be one of these near you, and notices are usually posted in vets' surgeries.

Working Trials

This is a specialist field, and one in which Springers have had some success. If it is something that you feel you would like to try then the first stages are as for basic obedience, after which it would be best to join a club that has a section training for working trials.

Agility

This is great fun and is becoming very popular. Again, local training clubs tend to have weekly sessions and will welcome all comers.

This is not really something that you can train for at home as you will need a lot of expensive equipment. Your dog will need to have basic obedience training and it is not advisable to start asking him to jump things until his bones and ligaments are fully developed for fear of causing damage. If you are not sure when to start your dog jumping, seek advice from the trainer at your training classes.

Ringcraft

This is a craft, and one that becomes easier the more you do. Yet again, training classes are very useful not only to train and socialize the dog, but also to train you and give you the confidence to stand out there with your dog. Remember that it is the dog who is being judged, not you, but how you handle the dog can make the world of difference to how he appears for that short time that the judge is looking at him.

Newcomers generally find it embarrassing to be 'out there' being watched, but remember, no one will think badly of you for having a go.

Show Lead

The lead you show your dog on needs to be chosen carefully. It must not be too heavy or bulky, and if you find that you have to use a check-chain to keep him in order this needs to be a different one to that described in the previous chapter. A fairly fine-linked chain will be less bulky and, as you will want to be able to loosen it when standing him up for the judge to see, it will need to be quite long, with approximately 12in (30cm) of spare chain when pulled tight to your dog's neck. The lead attached to this chain should also be quite thin.

Whether you choose a chain or a slip the actual lead wants to be no wider than half an inch, or slightly less for a bitch, as she will be slightly smaller than a dog. I prefer to use leather leads, but if this is what you choose your lead will need to be softened before use. Do not be tempted to put leather dressing on it as this will probably discolour your dog's neck. When I buy a new lead I sit at night, in front of the television, flexing it between my hands until it becomes soft and pliable. Of course you may prefer one of the many types of nylon leads on the market, which come in a large selection of colours. Whatever type you choose, remember that you will want to be able to screw it up in your left hand when moving your dog, so it must be pliable and not too bulky.

In the Ring

This is very important. The judge will be on the lookout for his winners from the moment they enter the ring so do be aware. To enter the ring amongst a lot of other dogs, with your dog looking good and walking nicely whilst appearing relaxed and casual, is far more difficult than running up and down alone once or twice. Our breed is inclined to 'pace' when walking slowly, and although the Breed Standard allows for this, it does not look very attractive. Therefore you want to practise walking your dog slowly, as unless you arrive late you will look a bit silly running into the ring. Arriving late is, of course, rather bad manners.

I do not like stringing my dogs up, but if you have a dog who persistently paces, this is one way that you can sometimes stop him and still walk slowly. With the lead up high behind his ears – do make sure that his throat is tidy and not all pulled forward in front of the lead – it is possible to pull him just off his front feet a tiny bit, and thus change his stride. This is not easy and it takes a lot of practice but may be worthwhile to give a good first impression.

You may at this stage have to collect your ring number from the steward. If so, keep your dog standing quietly by your side. This is where socializing at ringcraft is useful: you do not want your dog trying to play with all the others, or even annoying them by sniffing at them. Get your number as quickly as you can in order that you can choose where you want to stand in the line of dogs. If you do not want to go first then do not let them push you into that position. This can happen very easily with everyone hanging back, particularly in puppy classes, where it is often quite difficult to settle a puppy for the judge to look at him if he has just had a jolly good time running round the ring.

Standing your Dog

Having entered the ring you now have to stand your dog in line with all the others. Be sure to give yourself enough room. The best

Mr Bob Jackson's Sh.Ch. Moorcliff Regent, clearly showing his good upper-arm angulation, lay of shoulder and bend of stifle.

way to be sure of this is to leave a reasonable gap between you and the dog in front of you, enough so that if the handler behind is crowding you it is possible to move forward, but not so much that someone else may cram themselves in to the space. Some people are fanatical about being seen either first or last, but in order to give yourself time to settle after moving round the ring together, the head of the line is not an easy place for a novice handler to be. On the other hand, the dog who goes last has to be stood up very quickly after moving, and it is easier to have more time to settle your dog.

You can practise standing your dog at home, and it should be practised from a very early age to give him the feel of the stance you want from him. He should be stood with his front legs hanging straight down from the elbow at the natural width at which they drop. The front feet should not be turning in or out. The back legs

117

should be slightly further apart than the front. From the hock to the ground the leg should be upright and the stifle should show natural bend. The hocks should not turn in or out. The head should be held with the fingers of your right hand fitting neatly in to the groove under his jaw and your thumb on the outside of his flew, so that his head can be gently held in the position you require. Should your dog be difficult to hold like this then move your thumb onto the top of his nose. This will give more control but will not look as attractive. The head should be brought forward as far as is comfortable for the dog, without pulling his whole body forward, and should be held high enough to allow for a nice arch of the neck. The top of his skull should be parallel to the ground.

Your left hand should support his tail in a position to follow the set, again parallel to the ground. Sometimes the dog's markings are such that he may look better facing in one particular direction. This is quite permissible but it is advisable to practise on both sides as the judge may ask you to turn round.

You will walk into line with your dog on your left side and the lead in your left hand. Bring him to a halt and command him to stand, loosen the lead on his neck so that it falls on the point of his shoulder and lies with the angle of his shoulder. If you are confident that he will not run off, lay the lead on the floor and put your foot on it. If you want a little more control, transfer the lead to your right hand and loop it over your thumb. Take hold of the head in the right hand as previously described, at this stage holding with your thumb on top of the nose. Position his front legs, if necessary, with your left hand. I find the best way is to take hold of the leg at the elbow and reposition it to where I want it. Then, by holding the hock, or underneath the stifle, place the back legs as you want them. Check that the front end has not moved as you have done this, and that the front legs are still vertical. Now support the tail gently from underneath, and finally change your hold on the head if you can. This needs lots of practice at home for the benefit of both you and the dog. Just one or two stands a day will do; it will soon become second nature to both of you.

Keep your dog in this position until the judge starts to look at the first dog individually or asks everyone to move round the ring together.

118

Individual Assessment

When it is your turn to be seen, bring your dog forward while the previous dog is moving, if possible. This way you can stand him up, as previously described, at your leisure. Should this not be possible, be aware that your dog is in the judge's view from the moment he leaves the line, and remember what was said about entering the ring. Do not allow yourself to become flustered by the fact that the judge is watching you stand your dog. Provided you have practised thoroughly you should be able to stand him quietly and efficiently.

The judge will view your dog from every angle, so it is useful for him already to be familiar with people walking round him without him being allowed to move. It is also useful to stand your dog up in front of a mirror at home, so that you can see just where his feet should be placed to show him off to his best advantage. The judge will then come to his head, ask his age and look at his teeth, which should not present a problem provided your dog is used to his teeth being looked at. The less you say in front of the judge the better but, if you consider it necessary, it is permissible to use the command 'Teeth' at this stage. Whilst the judge is looking at your dog's head he should keep it still without it being necessary for you to hold it. As the judge moves on to assess the rest of the dog you will need to move forward to take your dog's head between your hands, bringing the ears forward as you do so, to allow an unrestricted view of his neck and shoulders. Again, here you can see the need for the stay exercise and, should you feel it necessary, you may give the command 'Stand' or 'Stay'.

After the judge has gone all over your dog, quietly move back to holding him from the side, making sure that the lead is still in the correct place on the shoulder and that his feet are still where they should be. The only exception to this is if the judge has repositioned one or more of his legs. Should this be the case assume that the judge knows best and leave them there.

Moving

When the judge has finished going over your dog he will ask to see him move. Do not be rushed. Reposition your lead to where you want it on your dog, and roll the rest of the lead up in your left hand so there are no loose, flapping bits. Personally, I like to see a

119

dog move as one with his handler on a loose lead. This is not always easy but worth working towards. The judge will instruct you on how he wants you to go, whether it is straight down and back or in a triangle. You will have practised both, and by the time you are in the ring you and your dog should be moving with confidence together at a pace that shows your dog off at his best. Different dogs look better at different speeds and it is important that you get someone to watch you and help you to find the right speed for your dog. Remember that puppies are bound to be a little over-enthusiastic at times, which is understandable.

If you have a dog who persistently paces, even when moving faster, it sometimes helps to swing him (not literally) round behind you as you move off at a trot; this seems momentarily to alter his balance, and the result will often be that he does not pace. If you have a dog who persists in pulling then go back to heel work on a check-chain and teach him to move at heel at the speed that you would show him at. Do remember when moving to go in straight lines and to try to come directly back to the judge. It is very annoying when you are judging to be hopping around the ring trying to get yourself into a position from where you can assess the dog's movement.

It is very nice, on coming back to the judge, if your dog will run into a show stance. This is not easy to achieve with a puppy, but there is no reason why the older dog should not learn to do this. You will need to let the lead tighten slightly as you slow down, and give the command 'Stand'. As you do so your dog should stop in a show stance. You can practise this at home and with time you will learn how to guide him into the correct position with a little pressure on the lead in a certain direction. This is much easier to do if you have the lead up high behind the dog's ears and have been stringing him up on the move, as you will have a firmer control over him. This does not look very nice in the ring, but there is nothing to stop you practising like this at home and then slackening off the lead as your dog understands what you want.

The Final Line-Up

Remember which dog was the first to have been seen by the judge and, as he is going over his last dog, start to stand your dog up ready for the final assessment. Do remember that you need to keep one eye on the judge and the other on your dog. The chances are that the judge will look at the whole line-up and then have another close look at each dog individually. He may even have you move again individually or all together around the ring. Whatever, keep on your toes but do not overtire your dog; puppies get bored easily and you do not want to put yours off at the very start of his career. If it is a very big class, once the judge has moved past you down the line, give your pup a little rest and a bit of fuss and then set him up again before the judge's eye comes back to you.

Keep an eye on the judge when he is calling out his final dogs, but do not stare at him. There is nothing worse for a judge than having an exhibitor daring him not to pull them out; I think it would have the opposite effect on most judges! If you are fortunate to get to the final few, again, keep calm, move as swiftly as you can to your place in the line-up, and stand your dog up again, it is not necessarily all over yet. Some judges will still change the places round after they have pulled out their final dogs.

Do remember that while you are in the ring your dog is on show, and always be aware that the judge may be glancing in your direction when you are not expecting it.

Whatever the outcome, you are taking home your 'best dog'. Leave the ring with a smile and be pleasant to the other exhibitors. If the chance presents itself congratulate the winner, without getting in the way, and hope that you have learnt from the experience.

The Show Dog Working Certificate

With the introduction in 1958 of the title Show Champion it became necessary for gundogs to qualify to gain their full title of Champion, and so the Show Spaniels Field Day came about. Any Spaniel who has won a first prize at a show where Challenge Certificates are on offer to that breed can compete at the Field Day, whereas any Spaniel who has won at least one Challenge Certificate can compete either at the Field Day or at a field trial to gain his Certificate. If you choose the second option you will be allowed to run your dog either in the lunch break or at the end. You will not actually have to enter the field trial, but it is still necessary to inform the secretary of the trial of your intentions. For the Qualifying Certificate your dog will be required to hunt, face covert, and retrieve game tenderly. He must not be noisy while in the line, and should not be gun-shy. It is not essential that he is absolutely steady, which helps.

121

The temptation when training for this is to think that practising with dummies will do; it will not. The judges have had the decency to give up their day to come and judge the dogs and the least you can do is to put your dog before them as well trained as possible. Far too few dogs who attend the Field Day get their qualifier, and the main reason for this is that they have not been prepared properly.

It is possible to teach your dog to quarter almost anywhere, provided he has some natural instinct and is basically obedient. The judges will not be looking for the style and speed found at a field trial. You can teach him to retrieve and to be steady to gun-shot, using a dummy and a starter pistol, if that is all that you have access to, but you really must make an effort to let him see some live game and have the opportunity to retrieve something that has been shot – even if you have to buy it cold from the butcher's. The game used for the qualifying test is not always freshly shot.

It really is worth the effort to have a go at the Show Gundog Working Certificate (formerly known as the Qualifying Certificate). After all it is what our dogs were originally designed to do, and the feeling of pride and satisfaction when you see your dog coming back with a difficult retrieve is indescribable.

Working Tests

Working tests are great fun and, unlike field trials, continue all the year round as dummies are used rather than live game. They can take place in a more confined space than a field trial, and without the need for live game, ground is easier to find for them. They could, I suppose, be classed as a cross between an obedience test and a field trial, and if you have your dog trained to a reasonable degree of obedience, he has a good nose (as he may be required to find a hidden retrieve), and he is not gun-shy, as guns are fired with blank cartridges, then you may like to have a go at some at the Country Fairs and Game Fairs held throughout the summer.

Field Trials

To train a dog for field trials is a very specialized job, which is why we find many people in this country specializing in doing just that. I will endeavour to outline below methods of training an English

F.T.Ch. Lewstan Paul retrieving pheasant to owner-handler Mr
Harry Hardwicke, 1973/74 season. Judges are Dr Tom Davidson and
Mr Andrew Wylie.

Springer for working, be it for competition or shooting for fun. Do bear in mind that this is a very specialist field and obviously each dog will vary greatly, making it difficult to generalize on how quickly to progress through the training programme.

The field trial English Springer of the 1990s is, on the whole, a gentle, biddable dog, willing to please and easily put down. The methods I shall outline will be to suit this type of dog. If your dog is of the harder, more boisterous type, then it will probably be necessary to start off in a different way, possibly by following the guidelines for basic obedience training, as given in Chapter 4.

The First Six Months

Having chosen your puppy, one that you are confident will enjoy retrieving, you will take him home and let him grow up a little. It is generally considered best to have a working dog kennelled, rather than living in the house where demands are made on him by the whole family. Bad habits can easily be picked up, such as playing ball or tug-of-war with the children, which are not good for a dog who you want to be steady and to retrieve tenderly later in life.

During this time, you and your puppy should be developing an understanding of each other and forming a bond. The puppy will learn to walk on the lead and to come when called, but very little more will be done in the way of training. The occasional casual retrieve can be practised, just to be sure that he has not lost interest in this very important part of later training. Little walks in the country to get him used to what will become his work place, are not training as much as part of the development of a relationship between you and your dog.

Six to Twelve Months

At six months old your dog may be ready to venture into more interesting things, but do be prepared for the fact that he may not, and remember to be patient. His natural tendency to hunt will be apparent, and as you are walking with him loose, keep him within a controllable distance of you. Remember that your voice is all-important in training. Do not get flustered, and if he strays just that bit further than you want him to, call him back using his name. If he ignores you, then harden your voice and call again. As soon as he is coming towards you soften your voice and encourage him in with praise. If he takes some time to come to you, do not be tempted to punish or chastise him when he does finally arrive: this will serve only to discourage him from coming quickly next time. This basic control will pay dividends later, and so time spent now is well worthwhile. There should not be anything formal about what you are doing with your puppy; just let him do what comes naturally and call him in to you as and when you wish. Do remember the praise and that the tone of voice is all-important. The quieter you can be with your dog, the more impact a sharp command will have when you do need to use it.

It is important that an English Springer has the confidence and ability to hunt freely and retrieve well, so these two things must be of paramount importance in the early stages of your dog's development. Before any more formal training is started be sure that he is retrieving and hunting well.

Retrieving a dummy to hand.

You can teach him to retrieve with a dummy that is preferably carried out of sight in a pocket. Hold your dog or put him on a lead while he watches you throw the dummy. Let him go for it on command, and then try to keep quiet until he has it safely in his mouth and is on his way back to you. Then, and only then, you can encourage him in. If you give too much encouragement while he is going for the dummy you can easily distract him from the task at hand, and if you praise him just that split second too soon, as he is picking up his retrieve, he can easily think that you want him back without it. You can test your dog's memory by throwing the dummy back while he is watching, and then carry on working him on forward. In your own time you can then send the dog back for the dummy. It is hoped that he will have remembered where it went and hunt back to it. Should he not remember, or in fact should any retrieve get missed, then quietly work your dog on towards that retrieve, and once he gets wind of the dummy he should find it. Do not be tempted to overdo the amount of times you allow your dog to do a retrieve, often just one will be enough. Do not sour him and always finish on a good note.

Once you are totally happy that he is hunting on with confidence and retrieving well then, and only then, can you progress with his training. There is no hard and fast rule dictating the age at which your dog will be ready to move on to the introduction of the whistle and basic obedience. Do remember to be sure of the hunting and retrieving first. Once you start to incorporate obedience you may well slow your dog down a little and if you slow him down too much by starting before he is hunting freely, you could well finish up with a dog who is too slow.

The commands you choose to use for your training are entirely up to you, and it really does not matter as long as the tone of your voice is right and you use the same commands for the same exercises every time. Also, the types of whistles you can use vary, and some people use two different whistles, one louder whistle to stop the dog and another quieter one to call the dog in. Again, the choice is yours, but be consistent.

Sit

The next step is to teach your dog to sit on command. Having competed in obedience competitions many years ago, I naturally use the command 'Sit', and so this is the command I shall use for the next stage. With your dog on the lead and walking by your left side, when you come to a halt use the command 'Sit', at the same time bringing the lead up in your left hand and showing the dog the raised palm of your right hand. Hopefully, he will sit. If, however, he simply has no idea of what you want, you might need to put your lead into your right hand and, as you bring the lead up, put some pressure on his quarters using your left hand and give the command 'Sit'. If you have to use this method, then four or five times of doing it should be enough for your dog to realize what you want and then you can go back to stage one. Provided you can think quickly enough the next time you come to a halt, bring up the lead in the left hand, give the command 'Sit' and give one quick toot on your whistle in quick succession. Continue with this exercise four or five times a training session for the next week, gradually changing the routine so that the whistle comes before the verbal command. By the second week you should not need to use the pressure of the lead any more, but do not be tempted to try this off the lead until you are confident that your dog understands fully what is required of him, and you are happy that his response is instant.

You can now progress to the sit exercise off the lead, allowing your dog to hunt round you and commanding 'Sit' by voice, or whistle, or both, and re-enforcing the command by showing the palm of your hand. This exercise is most important, as the essence of controlling your dog is being able to stop him wherever he may be. If you are not happy then put him back on the lead and go back to the earlier part of sit training. It is much better to spend a little time getting it right now, than having an unreliable dog later.

Please do remember that if you allow your dog to go on long enough to get bored he will lose concentration, and then you will lose the dog.

Polishing Up the Retrieve

By now your dog should be hunting freely under control, stopping on the whistle and retrieving happily. So now it is time to start some steadiness training.

A good way of training your dog to be steady on the retrieve is to place yourself between the dog and the dummy. This way you have more control. For example, allow your dog to hunt out a little way in front of you and then sit him using the whistle. Once he is sitting steadily take the dummy from your pocket and throw it behind you. All the time this is happening keep a hand up re-enforcing the command to stay, and if you think there is the slightest sign of your dog moving re-enforce the command further with the whistle or, if need be, your voice. Now walk forward to your dog, being very sure that he does not move, and in your own time (not his) send him for the dummy. If he should move slightly before this just take him back quietly and put him back where he was. If he moves persistently, he is not yet ready for this exercise and needs to go back to the sit.

When he brings in the dummy, presuming that he has waited nicely for your command, praise him and take it from him gently. Do not overdo this exercise – one or two good retrieves is far better than six bad ones – and do not let him get over-excited or bored.

The blind retrieve – one where your dog has not seen the dummy being dropped or thrown – will, it is hoped, follow on easily, with your dog's nose proving to be reliable. Working your dog in long grass, where the dummy cannot easily be seen, is a good way to introduce this exercise. Let your dog hunt on in front of you, and then as you walk along simply drop the dummy in the long grass without your dog seeing it go. If you then walk on a little further you can turn round and send your dog to hunt the ground where the dummy was dropped. He should then use his scenting powers to locate the dummy and so achieve the retrieve.

Hand Signals

You have already started your hand signals with the flat hand in the sit, and as your dog is progressing with his retrieve so you will need to direct him sometimes. Be sure that you make your hand signals clear. You will probably feel that the movements of your arms may be excessive, but remember that later on it could be that your dog is a long way from you in heavy cover and the 'larger' your hand signals are, the easier it will be for him to see them. Practise them: the more at home you feel doing them the better. They should come as a natural reaction when the situation calls.

Sitting to Shot

This should not prove to be a difficult exercise, provided the earlier exercises have been completed thoroughly, and your dog is not nervous of loud noises. A starting pistol is useful for the introduction of this exercise, as it is small and easy to carry, but can make a loud bang if loaded with the right caps. Let your dog hunt out a little way in front of you, and when you are ready blow the whistle for a sit and immediately afterwards fire the shot. Watch your dog to see that he remains sitting and does not look distressed. If it is clear that he did not like the bang, do not repeat the exercise until you can get someone to help you: the assistant can stand further away with the gun while you reassure the dog until he gets used to it. As soon as he has sat steady then praise him by walking out to him where he is. This can be repeated three or four times if you wish, but, yet again, remember that if it is going well do not repeat the exercise so much that it bores him.

The Rabbit Pen

A rabbit pen is basically an enclosed area of ground, in which rabbits are housed for the purposes of training your dog to hunt and flush (but not actually catch) game.

You may be fortunate enough to have access to a rabbit pen

Working in the rabbit pen.

belonging to a friend; if not, it is not difficult to construct one although materials can be expensive. A disused grass tennis court makes an ideal area for a pen, although not everyone will have access to one of those. However, the pen's area should be at least 11 sq. yd (10 sq. m), and an area larger than this is far preferable, although it will inevitably cost more to construct.

The pen must be fenced with fine wire netting, the base of which should be buried in the ground to prevent the rabbits from digging their way out and foxes and other predators from digging their way in. The fence must be high enough to prevent animals from jumping in (or out); and as a further precaution the top 12in (30cm) should be angled outwards, which should thwart most predators' attempts to gain access by climbing.

It does not matter if the area used does not have natural cover. You can add this yourself using cut branches, brambles and so on. The rabbits will also need somewhere to live: if you wish you can put a hutch in the pen and shut the rabbits in at night as an extra safeguard against predators; otherwise, an upturned feeding trough (of the sort used for feeding sheep) with one end raised to allow access, will give good cover, especially if cut brambles are then placed over it. You must also be sure that the rabbits are provided with a regular supply of fresh water and food.

It is not necessary to go out and catch wild rabbits; a few liberated from the pet shop will do quite well. By the time you take your dog into the pen, he should be steady enough for you to be able to ensure that the rabbits are safe, but it is important to provide some escape routes for them in case the dog should get carried away with his enthusiasm for the chase. Some lengths of drain-pipe set about the pen will serve the purpose.

Do not be tempted to enter the rabbit pen if you are not totally confident of your dog's steadiness. Accidents may happen, but are to be avoided at all costs. It is far better to take another month or six weeks on your training than to have your dog catch a rabbit. When he flushes a rabbit get after him quickly and strongly, and as soon as he has worked away from that rabbit, under your direction, give him lots of praise. Never let him hunt on in the direction that the rabbit has gone; always make him hunt the other way. Try not to get after your dog too much. Even though you will be tense and your dog excited by the fresh smells in the pen, try to allow him to hunt but be sure that he is under control at all times.

Introducing Game

Pheasants and rabbits can be stored in the deep freeze and brought out and defrosted at any time of the year. This way you can train your dog on game, be it cold game, at any time. This is obviously quite different to the dummies your dog has been used to, although some people do start by introducing dummies that are covered in rabbit fur, or that have feathers bound to them.

This is a very important time, and you will be keen that your dog accepts game, but do not let these tense feelings pass to your dog. This is something different for him and should be introduced quietly and as casually as possible. Just throw your bird a short distance and send him for it with lots of encouragement, then hope. If he is reluctant to pick it up, go to him, do not let any tension show, tell him what a good boy he is and just toss the bird a little further. Seeing you handle the bird, and the prospect of another retrieve (something which, by now, we know that he enjoys), should inspire him sufficiently to make him pick the bird up. If not, try using a rabbit, or even simply give him a retrieve with a dummy, so that

Ch. Mompesson Remember Me, top-winning show-bred English Springer of all time in the UK, proving that she is not just a pretty face.

you can finish on a good note and come back to this exercise another day. The important thing is that he does actually retrieve so, if need be, let him run straight in for his bird if you think that will help.

Negotiating a Fence

Some dogs take to jumping a fence quite naturally. Others may need a little encouragement to learn how to do it. This may mean you climbing backwards and forwards over the fence with him to give him the idea and the confidence. Once he has this idea and is jumping over happily then you can give him a short retrieve over the fence. This should not prove a problem, merely a natural progression.

Water

As with jumping, some dogs take to water readily, while others are

131

Sally, an English Springer happily re-homed by the English Springer Spaniel Welfare, demonstrating a retrieve from water.

more cautious, and this is not really somewhere that you want to go first!

A fine day is the first essential, after which you need to try to find a pond or lake with gently sloping sides for your dog's first introduction to water. Still water is better than running, as the current could be off-putting. Throw your dummy just a very short way into the water at first, and gradually throw it further and further in to deeper water as your dog gains more confidence, so that he is eventually swimming. Again, move on slowly, not doing too many retrieves on one day. Probably do not ask for swimming the first day; if your dog is confident make perhaps the second retrieve of the second day one where he has to swim. Progress slowly and do not overdo it. Do not give your dog the chance to fail: if you throw the dummy in too far, then throw him a nearer one so that he can be sure of finishing on a good note.

Steady to Game

As with the rabbit pen, this is a case of moving forward slowly and with great caution. The most important thing here is to introduce your dog to flapping, feathery things without him having the chance to catch one. Provided all your early training has been thorough enough this should not be a problem, but the temptation will be great for a young dog. You must be on the ball, ready with a sharp command when necessary, and lots of praise when he has turned his head away from temptation.

Getting it all Together

The moment when you and your dog can go out with a gun for the real thing should now be here. Try to take someone with you to do the shooting so that you can concentrate on your dog. Provided all the above stages have been covered thoroughly, you should both have a pleasant morning out. Again, do not overdo things at first. Two or three flushes, hopefully with a retrieve, should be plenty and if you feel that your dog is getting over excited then stop, let him sit quietly for a while to settle, and then decide whether you are going to let him fetch the bird or not. It is good for a young dog to work alongside an older dog who has experience, but do watch him very closely when the other dog goes for his retrieve, as the temptation will be very great for him to go too.

Hopefully, you and your dog will now be able to progress with time and experience and have many happy years working together.

The above has been a very brief outline of one way to train your English Springer. There are many excellent books on the market which are dedicated to this subject; we do not have enough space here to go into quite as much detail. There is also an excellent video available, which is filmed with Mr Harry Hardwicke, and demonstrates how to train an English Springer very clearly.

Different Countries' Individual Requirements

Great Britain

In the UK field trials are limited to sixteen dogs running on any one

The England Gundog Team for the International Working Tests at the CLA Game Fair in 1990. Left to right: Bob Wilkinson, Harry Hardwicke, Ian Openshaw, Andrew Ling and Jack Davey.

day, and dogs are numbered, and are under two judges who walk forward in line with four guns. The right-hand judge starts off with the odd numbers and the left-hand judge with the even numbers. When the judge on the right has worked his way through all of the odd numbers, he then sees the even numbers that are still in (have not been disqualified), and likewise the judge on the left then sees the odd numbers. In this way, both judges see all of the dogs hunt and, hopefully, all dogs will get two retrieves, one under each judge. This process will take all day, and dogs can be worked in varying covert: sometimes root crops, sometimes woodland with varying undergrowth, sometimes reeds, sometimes white grass or moorland or rough ground. At the end of the day the judges will compare notes, and often a run-off will be needed to decide the winner.

The USA

Dogs running in field trials in the USA are guaranteed equal opportunity to hunt and retrieve, as game is released for them. As in the UK, dogs work independently in pairs on a parallel course. Each dog and handler are accompanied by an official gunner and a judge. All dogs who perform well under the first judge are called back to compete again under a second judge.

The cover in the USA tends not to be as heavy as in the UK, and the Americans like their dogs to run bigger, wider and faster than the British do. In fact, the Americans favour the 'jump-into-the-air', driving flush that would be totally wrong in the UK. However, the dogs are often imported from the UK, or carry many British bloodlines, and are merely trained slightly differently.

Australia

The main game shot in Australia is rabbits, and one of the biggest differences, from the point of view of dog work between there and the UK, is the ground used. Paddocks (fields) are huge, and it is rarely possible to work them in strips as in the UK. The judge (there is only one to a pair of dogs) indicates the line of walk and usually zig-zags his way over the ground, often ignoring large areas; missing game is therefore not an elimination fault. Grounds usually hold a lot less game than in the UK, so that dogs have to work very hard for their finds. It would not be considered unreasonable for a pair of dogs to work for forty minutes or more for two or three finds. Bearing in mind that the handler has to do his own shooting, and that retrieving is one of the essential competencies evaluated, it is easy to see why the handler of any dog has to be a good shot and have excellent concentration, otherwise he has no chance of proceeding in the stake.

Organisers of field trials favour tussocky grassland or scrub for the trial site, as it is essential that the judge can see both dogs working. Because of this and the fact that the dogs always work in pairs, spaniels become very competitive and jealous, and when one dog puts up a rabbit and it is shot only feet from the other dog's nose and in full view, control has to be excellent.

The Continent

Field trials on the Continent tend to have a percentage of show-bred dogs, as well as field trial dogs, running in them. Terrain and game is variable, and handling perhaps not up to the standard of the UK.

Walter Harrisson judged at a field trial in the south of France in the late autumn of 1994 and his comments on returning were very interesting. He told me that the ground on which the trial was being held was on a hillside, where several other trials were also being held; he thinks that there were a total of eight. The ground had been under fire some five or six years previously and the cover varied from 6 inches to about 2 feet in height. Pheasants had been placed at first light in the area that was to be hunted, and only seven to nine dogs ran in a day as it was too hot to hunt in the afternoon. Dog number one went first, and so the card was worked through numerically. However, it was not worked through very quickly, as quite often a handler would be working another dog in one of the other trials, and when this happened one had to sit and wait for him to return, sometimes for up to three-quarters of an hour. About 60 per cent of the competitors were professional handlers, but Mr Harrisson did not feel that the standard of handling was very high; in fact he felt that the dogs were often better than their handlers. The dogs he judged had a lot of English blood, and quite a lot of English show blood was evident. Due to the lack of rabbits on which to train, the dogs tended to run with their heads up. The handlers were very noisy and tended to run to keep up with the speed at which their dogs were working. The retrieving standard was poor at this trial, and Mr Harrisson felt that the training was at fault: dogs were allowed to run in about 15 yards on a retrieve. At lunch-time a mobile pizza van and bar arrived on the hill with refreshments, and the pizzas were cooked within the van on an open, stone fire. A leisurely afternoon was had sitting about and discussing dogs with other judges and competitors. In the evening there was a dinner, and the judges sat on a long table opposite the handlers and filled out a type of dog's passport for each dog on their performance that day. The judges then had to stand up and address the room about each dog's performance, through an interpreter if necessary.

7

Showing

This should be fun. To some it is an all-consuming hobby, to some a pleasant day out with their much-loved pet, and to others a business. Throughout it all I can see no point in doing it unless it is fun, and this is important to remember: win or lose, at the end of the day you know that the dog you take home is still the best as far as you are concerned, and that is what matters.

For many people showing goes hand-in-hand with breeding, and at the end of the day the aim should be to breed a better dog, who will consequently win more in the show ring and eventually better the breed. Remember that what is done with dogs of today is passed on to the dogs of tomorrow.

Many people drift in to showing. They buy a puppy as a pet and then someone suggests that they show him. Others go out specifically to buy a show dog as they have decided that this is a hobby that they may enjoy. It is a most enjoyable hobby, where you will meet like-minded people and you can enjoy a day out with your dog – something that is becoming increasingly difficult to do with the anti-dog feeling that is about today.

You can travel as far as you wish to show your dog. There are many different types of show, starting with Exemption Shows and going through to Championship Shows.

Types of Show

Exemption Shows

This is the cheapest way of showing your dog, and is very useful for training both you and him. You will find such shows held all over the country throughout the summer months, often held in conjunction with fêtes and run for charity.

The body running the show must obtain a licence from the Kennel

Club to hold the show, and that is where any formality ends. As the name suggests, an Exemption Show is exempt from Kennel Club rules. You can enter your dog on the day of the show and he need not be registered with the Kennel Club. There are normally four pedigree classes: Puppy, Sporting, Non-sporting and Open, and from these classes a Best in Show (BIS) is found. Then follow the novelty classes: there are usually about six of these and they can be 'Best Crossbreed', 'Dog with the Waggiest Tail', 'Dog in Best Condition', 'Dog Most Like his Owner', 'Dog the Judge Would Most Like to Take Home' and so on. They are great fun and a very good place to learn and get over your ring nerves.

Primary Shows

These are run by a general dog show society or club, or a breed society or club. They are held in an evening or during a weekend, always starting after 2 p.m. No dog who has won a Challenge Certificate or Reserve Challenge Certificate, or a first place in anything other than puppy classes is allowed to compete, and all owners of the entrants must be members of the club or society holding the show.

Sanction Shows

Again, these are held for club or society members with the stipulation on entry here being that your dog must not have won his way out of the post-graduate class.

Limited Shows

Again, these shows are run by clubs and societies, usually for their members. This time the stipulation is that the show is limited to dogs who have not won a Challenge Certificate or any other award that counts towards the title of Champion.

Open Shows

As the name suggests, these shows are open to all. Yet again, they are run by canine clubs and societies. As you move up the scale of shows, so the entry fees get more expensive. The entry fee at an open show, however, is only about one-third of the entry fee at a championship show, and it is well worth polishing up your handling skills and your dog's behaviour having fun at these shows before setting sail for a Championship Show.

Championship Shows

These are shows where Challenge Certificates (CCs) are on offer, for most, but not always all, breeds. You will normally have to travel a distance to get to these shows, as they are held all over the country, on an average of once a week.

How to Find Out about the Shows

Advertisements appear in the dog papers every week for shows held all over the country. The bigger the show the longer before the show that entries close. So, if you see that there is to be a Championship Show in your area in June and, as it is local, you think that you may make it your first show at this level, you will need to be looking in the paper for adverts for the show in March, and entries will probably be closing in April. Show secretaries greatly appreciate a stamped, addressed envelope for schedules and you will find that once you have entered a show one year the schedule will automatically be sent to you for the next year.

When to Try the First Show

We have already talked about ringcraft classes in Chapter 6. You will find that the people at these classes are only too happy to advise you, not only when they think that you and your dog are ready for your first show, but also about which show would be suitable. Often, schedules will be available at ringcraft classes for all types of shows, and several people from the classes will be going along, so you will not find yourself totally alone.

The classification (classes on offer) at each show may vary slightly from show to show. You will find definitions of the classes listed in the schedule, together with the show rules and the regulations for the preparation of dogs for exhibition. Do read these carefully and if there is anything that you do not understand, do not be frightened to ask at ringcraft or give the breeder of your dog a ring. We all had to learn at some time and no one minds being asked. Assuming that you are starting to show your dog as a puppy, then obviously the Puppy class is the one to enter. At my puppies' first couple of shows I usually only enter them in one class per show, as I feel that they are there to enjoy themselves and I do not believe in over-showing puppies. It is best to let them enjoy their day out and try not to put them off by too much formality. You will hopefully be showing them for the next seven or eight years and you do not want to put them off now. If you are at all in doubt about what to enter, yet again, do ask.

What to Take to the Show

I have a bag that is my 'show bag' and in it live all of the things that I may need at a show. If I have to take anything from the bag to use it at home, then as soon as I have used it I put it back in the bag. This way when I get to the show I know that I will have everything I need. The only exception to this is a bottle of water, which obviously gets put in last thing before leaving home. No matter what type of show you are going to you may find that you need any of the following things:

A benching chain and collar, three different types of slip lead, plus a chain slip and lead.

A comprehensive grooming kit should include paw wax, a hard brush, anti-static coat gloss, two types of grooming glove, a rake, grooming stone, a soft brush, two combs with different teeth, a pair of straight scissors, a pair of scissors with one straight and one jagged edge and finally a pair of scissors with two jagged edges.

Everyday lead
Show lead (I take two, just in case)
Ring clip
Grooming kit
Pad wax (this goes on the bottoms of your dog's feet if the floor is slippery)
Wound powder
Collar (with name tag)
Benching chain
Large piece of fleecy bed or blanket
Towel
Water bowl
Water
A bag of doggy treats
Rescue Remedy (very useful for settling the nerves of dog or handler)

I also take a folding chair, as seats are usually scarce at dog shows. A picnic lunch and a drink can be a good idea. A large folding cage can also be an asset at unbenched shows.

Preparing Your Dog for the Show

I am a great believer in preparing your dog at home and only having to give him a quick brush up at the show.

You will have been getting him used to being groomed and handled but, as your first show nears, serious trimming may well be necessary. Different puppies' coats grow at different speeds, and it may be that your puppy does not need very much trimming for his first show, but he is still bound to need some. I do not like to see English Springers over-trimmed and do not believe in using clippers on them. The most important thing to remember, in my opinion, is that when you have finished trimming him, your dog should look natural. You want to emphasize his good points and minimize his bad points, while producing a dog who looks healthy in coat, with good lines, and with no obvious chunks cut or clipped out.

1. Start at the **head**. Never use clippers or scissors here. Any dead or loose hair on the cheeks or top of the head should be plucked out with your forefinger and thumb.
2. Tops of the **ears**. Here, the thinning scissors can be used together with a large-toothed comb. With the scissors held vertically, thin the hair at the top of the ear to about one-third of the way down. After every three or four cuts run the comb through to remove loose hair. It is better at this stage to take off too little than too much; over-trimming here can cause the new hair to grow through discoloured. If in doubt, ask the breeder or someone else with experience of the breed.
3. The **lower part of the ear** should only need combing through in a puppy but, as the dog gets older, it may be necessary to thin this slightly. It is sometimes necessary to trim round the bottom of the ear flap if it is straggly, or if it is getting too long and pendulous. If it is necessary to trim round the end, then use the thinning scissors, and leave the ear so that it will reach about 1 inch beyond the end of the nose, when pulled forward.
4. **Inside the ear flap** needs trimming to help it lay flat to the head,

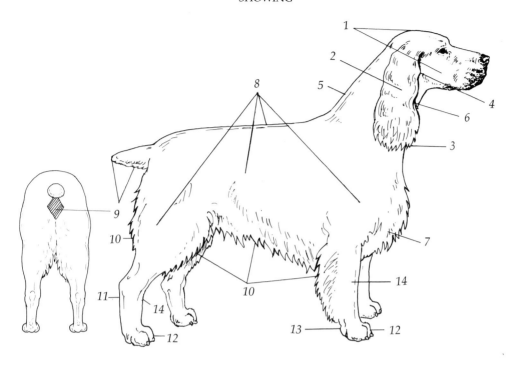

Trimming.

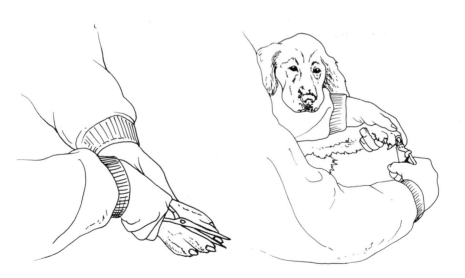

Do not cut across the growth of the hair when trimming between the toes.

Trimming the toe-nails with guillotine clippers.

143

and to allow air to reach the ear canal without obstruction. Trim around the opening to the ear canal to about half an inch all of the way round. Again, if in doubt do ask.

5. The **top of the neck** should be combed through and if there is any dead hair it should be removed using finger and thumb.

6. **Under the chin** down to the **breast bone** should be trimmed with the trimming scissors. Again, have them pointing downhill, at a slight angle, and trim with the hair until you have a smooth, natural effect. Trim off more here than you did from the top of the ears. The piece that you trim will be about 6 inches wide, and the neck hair that joins each side of this area should blend in naturally with the hair you have trimmed.

7. The **feather below the breast bone** that goes down between the front legs to join the tummy feather should be left alone on a puppy. It may be necessary, on an older dog, to take some of it off at some time if it gets very thick and heavy, but you can take advice on this when it is appropriate.

8. The top of the **back** and **sides** should never be touched with the scissors. Any dead hair should be removed using finger and thumb or combed out with a medium-toothed comb or a rake.

9. The **tail** should be tidied up underneath, as shown on the shaded area on page 143, with the thinning scissors, again so that it blends in naturally. It is also usual to trim along under the tail and to take any hair off the end. The top of the tail is treated as a continuance of the back. If your dog has a long tail, then trim around the anus as described. You may also find that you need to tidy up the lower line of the feather on the tail, as you would for a setter.

10. The feather on the **quarters**, the **front legs** and **under the tummy** of a puppy should not need any trimming, but you may find that it will need some thinning and shaping later in life.

11. From the **hock** to the ground on the back leg should again be trimmed with the thinning scissors held vertically to create a natural, tidy appearance.

12. The **feet** should be trimmed round with the straight scissors to emphasize the tight, round foot that we require. The hair from the underside of the foot should also be trimmed flat to the foot, and the hair that grows between the toes should be trimmed off where it protrudes, so that the foot is smooth and neat. The toe-nails must, of course, be kept trimmed back.

13. From the floor to about 1 inch up the **back of the front leg** should be trimmed with the straight scissors.

144

English Sh.Ch. Chasmar Penny Farthing showing a lack of coat and feather.

14. Any dead hair on the legs should be plucked out using the finger and thumb.

15. The **teeth** should be kept clean and free from scale.

Awards – What You Can Win and What it Means

It is a good idea to keep a record of your wins at shows. This helps you to be sure when you have won your way out of different classes. As mentioned previously, each schedule prints the definitions of the classes and, provided you know how many wins you have had, it is quite easy to be sure to enter the correct class.

Around the world, different countries have their own requirements for making up a Champion or Show Champion, as outlined below:

145

UK

A dog who wins the Challenge Certificates (CCs) under three different judges, one of which must be when the dog is over twelve months old, is awarded the title Show Champion, and this is confirmed by the Kennel Club with a certificate. If the dog already holds, or should he subsequently gain, his Show Gundog Working Certificate then he may use the title Champion.

Southern Ireland

Dogs who reside in the UK may be shown in Southern Ireland provided they are registered with the Irish Kennel Club. Therefore, we sometimes find Irish Champions in the UK, as well as in Ireland.

To become an Irish Show Champion dogs must win forty green star points. Amongst these points must be four 'Majors' which are wins to the value of five points or more. The number of points awarded depends on the number of dogs present at the show. As in

Eire's top winner of all time, Sh.Ch. Skelsea Amber Solaire, owned by Mr and Mrs R. Hughes.

the UK, in order to hold the title Champion, a gundog must gain a qualifying certificate.

FCI Countries

Shows in most European countries and many other countries around the world are held under the auspices of the FCI (Federation Cynologique International), and with slight regional differences the requirements to make up a Champion are as follows – the CAC (Certificat d'Aptitude au Championnat de Beaute) is awarded to the best of each sex, provided that he or she has won his or her class and been graded excellent. There are some countries where dogs under a certain age and dogs already holding the title Champion cannot compete for the CAC, although they can compete for best of each sex and best of breed. The number of CACs required to make up a Champion varies from country to country, and in some countries dogs must be over a certain age before they can hold this title. In Belgium, France, Italy and Switzerland a Gundog Qualifying Certificate is required before a dog can hold the title Champion, and the work demanded for this certificate is more difficult than in the countries already mentioned.

Australia

This country is a total exception to what has been written above. Although a member of the FCI they judge almost to the English system and award CCs; however, it is not the number of CCs which count towards making up a Champion, but the points gained at shows. A total of 100 points must be gained to make up a Champion. Twenty-five points can be gained by winning a group, five points are awarded for winning the CC, plus one point for attending the show and another point for every dog your dog beats. It is important to remember that entries are often quite small and in fact it is possible to make up a Champion without ever competing against another dog, as the CC and point for attending are awarded even if your dog stands alone.

USA

Here, championship titles are also awarded on a points system and in order to become a Champion a dog must gain fifteen points,

Sh.Ch. Bowswood Barleycorn, owned and bred by Mrs M. Bower.

including two 'Majors' which are wins of three, four or five points each, and which must be gained under two different judges. The number of points varies between one and five, dependent on the show's location and the number of dogs competing. These points can only be awarded to dogs who are not already Champions and all class winners (except Champions) can compete. The highest number of points a dog can win at any one show is five, and he may be awarded extra points up to this number should he win Best of Breed or Best in Show. Once a dog has gained his title then he can only compete for Best of Breed, and competition for this is keen as it gives the opportunity to compete in the Sporting Group.

The Day of the Show

It would be very unusual if you were not nervous on the day of your first show; we all have been. Whether it is an Exemption Show

Sh.Ch. Windydale Whimsicle Ways at Calvdale, owned by Mrs N. Calvert and bred by Mrs S. Shaw.

or a Championship the thought of entering that ring will be daunting. Just remember that this is supposed to be fun, and you are here for you and your dog to have a nice day out, win or lose; that is what matters.

Hopefully you have got everything that you need from your check list, and your dog is clean and trimmed. If it has been necessary to give him a bath then this should have been done a couple of days prior to the show, to give his coat time to settle. Sometimes, when you give a dog a brush over at the show, his coat suddenly decides that it has a mind of its own and follows the brush. This is caused by static electricity, and used to be remedied by an anti-static spray; however, these sprays have recently been banned in the UK by the Kennel Club.

It is best to arrive at the show with plenty of time to let your dog get used to the strange surroundings and for you to find your way

Mrs J. Taylor's Sh.Ch. Cleavehill Yorkshire Spirit.

B.O.B. at Crufts 1995, Sh.Ch. Chaun Chablais at Lyndora with the owner Mrs D. Bury and judge Mr A. 'Geof' Nicholls.

150

Sh.Ch. Teesview Tumeric, owned by Mrs E. Dobson.

around. Provided you are not in the first class of the day, try to get the chance to watch the judging for a little while and see where the exhibitors are being asked to stand in the ring, which way they are moving their dogs, and whether you will be given your ring number inside the ring, or will have to find it from elsewhere. If it is a Championship Show the ring numbers are sometimes on the bench with the bench numbers. At smaller shows the numbers will be at the secretary's table, if they are not being given out in the ring.

Find yourself a suitable place to settle your dog down. Remember that if you are there with friends, it may be that your dog will pull towards them when he is in the ring, if he can see them. If it is a benched show introduce your dog to his bench carefully. When you attach him to the bench with his benching chain and collar (not a

The final line-up at the Northern English Springer Spaniel Championship Show, 1988. Left to right: Mrs Eunice Ward with Sh.Ch. Wardhill Whistling Miller (dog CC and B.I.S.); the Judge, Mr Doug Shepherd; Mrs Pat Guy with Sh.Ch. Fenaybrook Lady Madona (bitch CC and B.O.S.); and Mrs Lyn Gregory with Arcadia Augustus (Best Puppy in Show), who later gained his title.

check-chain or slip-lead), it must be the correct length, so that he cannot scramble off the bench and hang himself.

When it is time for your class, enter the ring quietly and with confidence. If you have to collect your ring number in the ring, the steward will have it, and you should already know what number you require. Try to stand somewhere midway down the line of dogs. This way you will have time to settle yourself and your dog before the judge gives you the individual inspection, and you will not have to rush back into line and stand your dog up immediately, which you would if you were the last dog to be seen.

Listen carefully to any instructions given to you in the ring by the judge or the steward, and do not get flustered. You have paid your entry fee, the same as everyone else, and you deserve your time in the ring. When the judge asks you to stand up your dog take your time to get it right, and when it comes to moving adjust the lead to where you want it on the dog's neck and move off in your own time. Do not be tempted to chat with the judge. This is not 'done';

152

*Am. Ch. Carousel's First Born Son, owned by Jeanie and Bill Legier,
and Sandie Pappa, seen here with English judge Mrs Pam
Wadsworth who awarded him his crown.*

153

the only conversation that should be necessary with the judge is to answer when he asks the dog's age.

Do be sure to move the way the judge has asked. He may want a triangle, or straight up and back, or both. You will have practised these things at ringcraft and they should not be a problem.

After the judge has seen all of the dogs, keep one eye on him so that you will notice if you are fortunate enough to be called out, but do not stare at him; this does not impress any judge and I think it may well put some off. If you are placed, accept the fact gracefully with a smile and a 'thank you'. If you can do it without getting in the way, congratulate the winners placed above you. If you are not placed, accept it even more gracefully and leave the ring with a smile. You know that you still like your dog best.

8

Judging and Stewarding

Getting Started

People come to judging from different aspects of the canine world: some come from showing and breeding successfully, others come from the administrative side (show secretaries and so on), and others from stewarding. In my opinion the best judges come from stockmen, people who have 'an eye'. This is something very difficult to define, but the owner of a successful kennel must have that extra something to be able to spot 'a good un' from a very early age. In their breed at least, this should give them the ability to pick out the best in a ring full of dogs, be it that their best will probably come from a very similar type to their own. Admittedly, some people are more academic than others, and this type of person is probably better equipped to come to judging through exams than the less academic among us.

Why Judge?

Some people never wish to judge, being much happier exhibiting their own dogs; others like to judge but prefer to exhibit; others start off as successful exhibitors and eventually become so in demand for judging appointments that this takes over from exhibiting; whilst others set out to judge with exhibiting merely being an introduction to the ring.

Amongst all of these different attitudes towards standing in the middle of that ring and giving your opinion, all but the first group of people have decided, at some stage, that this is what they want to do. It may sound rather self-opinionated to think that by being there and giving your view you can further the good of that breed, but let us face facts. The exhibitors are all there trying to win, and what the judges put up on a regular basis will influence the future development of the breeds, therefore what you do when you judge

155

The late Mrs A. Chedzoy-Davies, Judge at Windsor Championship Show 1981, with her B.C.C. and B.O.B. Mrs P. Shaw's Sh.Ch. Ardencote August Love and D.C.C. Mr G. Miller's Sh.Ch. Graftonbury Genghis Khan.

is just as important as what you are doing in your breeding policy.

Many judges get a sort of 'buzz' from seeing an exhibit they have placed highly go on to greater things. How often have you heard a judge comment 'That dog was my Best of Breed', or 'I gave him his first puppy class'? There is a sort of reflected pride in the wins of a dog who you thought highly of.

Some judges enjoy the social side of judging. Lunch out with self-minded people, even hotel accommodation and air fares are paid for some of the more prestigious shows. It can be quite an attraction for some people to make a hobby of judging, rather than showing.

How and When

Around the world, methods of qualifying to judge vary tremendously. Some countries have student judges, who watch alongside a qualified judge and have the opportunity to handle the dogs after

156

Judge Mrs O. Hampton in 1957 with her CC winners at Chester.
Mr J. Cudworth shows Ch. Mowgrain Mr Chips and Mrs
F. Sherwood Ch. Northdown Donna.

the judge has, and to ask the judge for comments on the dogs. This sounded to me at first like a very good idea but, having experienced it first-hand, now I am not so sure. I found that the student tended to get in my way: every time I stepped back I fell over someone else. It took far longer to assess the dogs with the student going over them after me and somehow I felt it interfered with my 'flow' of judging. There is also the danger that a strong-minded student judge will actually disagree with the judge, who might find himself having to defend his decisions.

Another way of judges being approved is by written tests, which seem to me to lean towards favouring the academics amongst us.

Judging seminars are becoming more and more popular and, provided the student judges have the opportunity for hands-on experience, I think that this is an excellent way to learn about a breed.

Stewarding for a respected breed specialist is another valuable way to gain knowledge, particularly if the judge will allow you to read the notes appertaining to the class winners.

There is nothing like getting out and doing it for concentrating the brain. Naturally, before embarking on your first judging appointment, you would have been to some seminars on the breed and would be completely familiar with the Breed Standard. Then, of course, the very act of standing in that ring and going over the dogs, trying to fit dog to Standard, is a wonderful teaching aid.

It is generally accepted that the first time you judge, it will be the breed that you keep and show, and that you will have been showing that breed for at least five years. It is not 'done' to go out looking for judging appointments. One day, if you have been showing good Springers and have displayed a genuine interest in the well-being of the breed, someone will put your name forward for a few classes at an open show, the secretary will contact you and off you will go.

There is a great temptation in this day and age to take on judging appointments for breeds you know nothing about. Show secretaries are trying to keep their costs down, and if they can get a judge to do more than one breed the expenses will be less. Do not be tempted. It is not fair on the exhibitors to judge dogs of whose breed you have no knowledge. The very experienced all-rounder may be able to read a Breed Standard, digest it, and then judge a fresh breed, but remember that he has probably been judging for a great many years and will have seen many good dogs from all breeds along the way.

What to Wear

This may seem petty, but it is important. Your clothes should set you apart a little from the exhibitors, without being completely over the top. It is far easier for the men than for us ladies; a smart pair of trousers and jacket with a shirt and tie, or a suit are just fine for men. Some young dogs are put off by someone wearing a hat; however, if the weather is inclement, then a hat and waterproof coat are quite acceptable for both sexes. For the ladies, I found the arrival on the fashion scene of culottes to be a real breakthrough. Here are 'skirts' we can wear without fear of them ending up round our necks at the first gust of wind. Again, a shirt and jacket look smart and are practical; or should it be a hot day, a blouse is fine, but try to avoid plunging necklines! I always pin up the tails of my judge's rosette, as these can be quite off-putting wafting in the faces of the dogs.

*Austral. Ch. Clanach Argyle Tartan, bred and owned by Mrs
P. Merchant, out of Austral. Ch. Cranboh Argyle and Oak Sword
Dancer.*

Conduct in the Ring

Unlike your first time in the ring exhibiting, this time everyone is watching you and everyone is ready to criticize! This is not a place for the weak-hearted. You are bound to be nervous, we all were, but this time you must accept that the ring is always surrounded by people with different opinions to the judge. There are only a small number of the people here who can win by the law of averages, and the most important person to please at the end of the day is yourself.

The temptation to be influenced by dogs or handlers that have done a lot of winning will be great, but do not let this happen. It is most important that you judge honestly. On the way home you must be able to look back over what you have done and know that it was for all of the right reasons. If you have made mistakes, let them be honest mistakes and learn by them.

Am. Ch. Canarch Soft Music, a black and white bitch owned by Mary Lee Hendee, handled here by B. Heckerman and pictured with judge Mr F. Hunt (see Appendix II for pedigree).

160

The ring is yours for the time you are in it, and without being aggressive, you should command that ring. How you conduct yourself is all-important; how ever you feel inside, appear confident and get yourself into a routine right from the start.

I did not know what to do with my hands on my first judging appointment and so I stuffed them in my pockets. I was told afterwards by a rather outspoken exhibitor that he considered it an insult to be judged by a judge walking around the ring with her hands in her pockets. I have never judged with my hands in my pockets since; I now tend to hold my hands behind my back!

Make use of your stewards but do not let them rule you. Decide where you want your new dogs to stand and where the dogs who have been seen should be, and be sure that the steward knows.

If you want all of the dogs to move round the ring before individual assessment then tell the exhibitors clearly, telling them how many times you would like them to go round.

If you want the next dog stood up, ready for you to go over, while you are watching the previous dog move, tell the steward.

When going over the exhibit, take your time. What you are seeing must be remembered to the end of the class. Walk round the dog and view him from every angle, then approach him gently, going to his head first. Ask his age (this will be the only conversation you have with the exhibitor unless you feel that the dog has an unsoundness), examine his teeth and the shape of his skull, eyes and ear set. Move on to the neck and then the shoulder. Feel for the shoulder and upper-arm placement; this can be deceptive with coat and markings, and your hands may surprise you. Check front legs and feet, noting how the elbows are set to the body. Look for width between front legs; again, feather can make this deceptive. Feel the spring of rib right across the body, and depth of body, length and strength of loin, and topline, noting the tail set. Check for two testicles in male animals (castrated dogs can now be shown in the UK, although it is rare), note strength of second thigh and bend of stifle, length from hock to ground and construction of quarters relating to propulsion.

Stand back and take another look at the complete dog, bearing in mind what you have found as you have gone over him. Then clearly instruct your exhibitor how you would like him to move his dog (by the end of judging you will wish that you had a record of this sentence). If the dog plays up, have him move again. It is better to be sure than to think that he moved all right.

161

After you have seen all of the dogs individually you should have a fair idea of what you like. If it is a very large class you may like to shortlist several dogs for consideration. If you do this, tell the exhibitors that this is what you are doing, and then dismiss the remaining dogs with a polite 'Thank you, I have finished with the rest.' At this stage you may like to see the shortlisted dogs move again or not, dependent on how well you can remember their movement. It is not very polite just to have one or two move again. It is better to start at the head of the line and see them all move. I always feel that if at all possible, it is better not to pull out your winning dog until you are quite sure that it is your winner; and if possible have the whole line up in your mind before calling any out.

Judge's Book

It is your responsibility to see that the judge's book is filled out accurately, and you have to sign every leaf to the effect that this is so. It is common practice to sign all of the book before judging starts, therefore saving time later. This is alright provided you are going to fill in the remainder of the book yourself and are confident that no mistakes will be made.

After the placings have been made and the results written down by yourself in your book and by the steward on his card, the first and second dogs will remain in the ring for you to make notes about them ready for writing your critique later. It is normal to make these notes in the space adjacent to the ring numbers of the winning dogs in the judge's book. Some judges have taken to speaking into a small tape recorder rather than writing notes. I normally write about the first and second prize winners, even at open shows, and hope that they may get printed although it has become practice for the papers only to print critiques on the class winners at open shows and just the names of second- and third-placed dogs.

Writing the Critique

To me, this is a most important part of judging. For a novice judge it is amazing what can be learnt when sitting down with rough notes on the winners and a copy of the Breed Standard. There may be small points where you find that you were criticizing or praising the wrong thing, and the very act of writing out a critique on a breed, with the aid of the Standard of that breed, will consolidate

162

Am. Ch. Salilyn's Condor, bred by Mrs Julia Gasow and owned jointly with Dr and Mrs Roger Herzig. His handler is Mr Mark Threlfall. 'Robert' was top-winning show dog in the USA in 1992 and took Best in Show at Westminster in 1993.

163

what you know about it, and possibly point out something that had not previously occurred to you.

Exhibitors appreciate knowing what you thought of their dogs: they would not have entered under you unless they had wanted your opinion, and even if their dogs were not placed, it is interesting for them to read why you placed the dogs that beat them.

In my opinion, the critique should be constructive not destructive, whilst being honest and to the point. In most cases when judging under FCI rules, a critique has to be written on every dog and an honest critique that accurately describes the dog is far more highly thought of than a flowery critique that could describe any dog. The first time I ever judged under FCI rules and had to write on every dog, I found it quite strange, although not unpleasant. What I did find quite amazing was the exhibitors flooding into the ring at the end of the class to collect their copies of the critiques, and then coming to see me at the end of judging to discuss them with me. There was no animosity: they greatly appreciated an honest assessment of their dogs and wanted to discuss how I thought they could improve on what they had. I find this attitude most refreshing, and although it would be impractical to implement this method of a critique for every dog in countries where very large entries are usual, I feel that it is a great loss to the exhibitors in those countries.

In the UK it is normal for only the class winner to get a critique from an Open Show, and first- and second-placed dogs to get one from a Championship Show, and not all judges are even doing this now. When you write a critique, it is usual to start at the head and work your way over the dog in a similar way to going over him when judging, considering teeth, eye and expression, head, neck, shoulder and so on. Throughout, your aim should be constructive criticism, combined with compliments where appropriate.

Important Points to Remember

Soundness is all-important. You are not expected to hold a veterinary qualification in order to judge, but it is absolutely necessary to be able to recognize an unsound animal.

Teeth

The requirements, as laid down in the breed standards, vary greatly

164

from breed to breed, and the requirements on teeth vary for our breed from country to country. In the UK we accept nothing less than a perfect scissor bite. In the USA there is a little leeway on this point. In most FCI countries the total number of teeth count, and sometimes they are actually counted.

Type

This is an emotive point, and one which many disagree on. 'Type' is that indefinable something; we all like a type, and when we are judging is it nice to end up with that type in our final line-up. However, whether we should allow faults to creep through in order to keep that type in our final line-up is a matter that is discussed at length, and will always cause disagreement.

This was mentioned previously, but is well worth a further mention: do remember that at the end of the day you are the person that you have to please. Your class winners should be the dogs that you like best and that, in your opinion, fit the Breed Standard better

Judging 'to type'.

than any others. Do not be phased, do not be influenced, make your own honest judgment and no one can have room for complaint. The highest compliment that can be paid to a judge is 'Well, I don't know what he will do, but whatever, it will be his honest opinion.'

When in Rome

When judging around the world, remember to check that the country in which you are judging uses the same Breed Standard as the country in which you are used to judging. The FCI uses the Breed Standard from the country of origin of the breed, in this case England. The USA has its own Breed Standard, and therefore when judging in the USA this Standard should be used, even by a judge who is used to judging to the British standard, and vice versa.

Stewarding

In some countries stewards have to qualify for their job. In other countries such as the UK they learn by experience, and often use the experience as an aid towards learning to judge.

If you are invited to steward and you have not done so before, be sure that you will have an experienced steward to work with, as it is a very responsible job and a judge's task can be made quite difficult if assisted by an inexperienced steward on whom he has to keep checking up. It is normal to have two stewards in a ring and their responsibilities are: to make sure that exhibitors are aware that judging is about to start; to announce the class number that is about to be judged and call exhibitors into the ring; to check that exhibitors are wearing their correct ring numbers; to mark off absentees in the judge's book; to tell exhibitors where the judge would like them to stand; to make sure that exhibits who have come forward from a previous class are standing apart from the 'new dogs', and are in the correct order with dogs who have been placed first in a previous class ahead of dogs who have been placed second in a previous class, and so on. Stewards must be ready to follow up any instructions that the judge may have given to an exhibitor who has not understood, perhaps one who has not left the ring when asked to, or has come forward into line in the wrong position. If the steward has any doubt on any of these things, the judge should be consulted. Stewards need to be ready to give the judge his judge's book and pen when he has made his final decision and wishes to write in the results. Stewards give out the prize cards and take the results independently of the judge. Where two stewards are working together, one will normally give out the prize cards and announce the winners, in a loud voice so that the spectators on the ringside can hear, while the other takes the results. A card, as illustrated here, is a very useful way of keeping a check on results and unbeaten dogs and bitches:

Class No.	Sex	1st	2nd	3rd	Res.	VHC	HC
1	D	72	68	54	80	73	56
2	D	79	72	68	49	36	56
3	D	86	72	49	50	68	20
4	B	55	73	69	54	57	61
5	B	63	73	67	54	61	62
6	B	82	63	73	61	84	90

By this process of elimination it is easy for the steward to see, at a glance, which dogs and bitches remain unbeaten at the end of judging. Therefore he knows which ones are eligible to compete for Best Dog and Best Bitch. It should be remembered that Reserve Best Dog and Reserve Best Bitch can come from second place, provided the dog or bitch who beat them has taken Best Dog or Best Bitch. This is at the judge's discretion, and the second-placed exhibit does not automatically have the right to compete.

If a steward is in doubt of the eligibility of any dog for any class, this should not become the judge's problem (the judge is there to judge what is put before him). The steward should quietly consult the show manager or secretary, whose duty it is to make such decisions on the day, although at a later date they may be referred to the Kennel Club.

Stewarding is undoubtedly a good way to learn and, by offering your services as a steward, you are helping out the society concerned; but do be aware that the job demands concentration, competence and confidentiality.

9

Breeding

Before embarking on breeding a litter there are many things to consider, such as: are you going to be able to find suitable homes for your puppies? Do you have the time, space and energy to rear a litter? Will you be able to cope if things go wrong and you have to rear an orphan litter? Do you really want a litter? These are all very important points and should be considered carefully. The very best reason for breeding a litter of puppies is because you want to keep a puppy yourself from your bitch. Whether she is a top show dog, a super worker or is simply your most faithful companion, it is quite understandable that you would like to perpetuate what you have in her. If you are competitive the challenge of trying to improve on what you have, in the next generation, is great, but do be prepared for the possible disappointment of the litter not turning out as you had hoped. This has happened to all of us at some time and, as long as you learn from your experience, all is not lost.

Never look to making money from breeding a litter of puppies or you will be disappointed. If you consider the cost of keeping your bitch for the twelve months that she goes between litters, the stud fee for the dog of your choice, the cost of rearing the litter, and any vet's fees that may be incurred along the way, these things alone would soon take up any income that you have from your litter, without the entry fees and petrol that you use going to competitions. Having said all this, it is very satisfying to breed a litter and see the joy they give their new owners: we receive many Christmas cards each year from dogs all over the world. Breeding is an enjoyable hobby, but it does involve some hard work along the way.

Breeder's Licence

In the UK, when you own two or more 'breeding bitches' you are required by law to have a breeder's licence, which is issued by your

A well suited breeding pair: Ch. Moorcliff Dougal of Truelindale and Sh.Ch. Slayleigh Paulina.

district council. The term 'breeding bitches' does not mean bitches who are being regularly bred from, but bitches who could be bred from: who have not been spayed. To obtain a licence you have to apply to your district council, and they will send a dog warden out to inspect your premises before a licence is issued. The annual cost of this licence varies from district to district.

The Brood-Bitch

Your first consideration should be whether your bitch is suitable to be bred from. Does she have a good temperament? Does she suffer from any hereditary defect, such as entropion or an incorrect bite? Has she been tested clear under the necessary health schemes and is she the right age to be bred from? All of these things should be considered carefully before mating a bitch. It is advisable not to breed from an English Springer bitch before her third season, by which time she will be almost fully mature. However, some bitches have their first season very late and may be ready for breeding from on their second season. If in doubt, consult your vet. It is advisable not to allow your bitch to have her first litter too late in life; I would say that five years old was plenty late enough for a first litter. If you want to keep a puppy from your pet and do not want it while your bitch is still very young, it may be best to let her have a litter at about two years of age, and sell all the puppies, and then breed another litter from her at six or seven years of age, from which you can keep a puppy. The Kennel Club in the UK will not register any puppies from a bitch who has whelped after eight years of age.

Your bitch should be in peak fitness when ready for mating. A

The outstanding bitch Sh.Ch. Slayleigh Paulina, who was not only a champion herself but produced six show champion offspring.

Pencloe Clearway at Feorlig at eight months old, owned by Mr and Mrs Don Miller. This bitch won her first CC at twelve months of age and, when an accident curtailed her show career, she proved to be a wonderful brood-bitch, producing four show champions and three more CC winners from three litters to three different sires.

fat bitch may easily not conceive, while, on the other hand, a bitch who is too thin and in poor health may reabsorb some or all of the foetuses.

The Stud-Dog

Choosing a stud-dog to suit your bitch is a very important decision and should be given a great deal of consideration. You should look at your bitch objectively. Do be honest with yourself: any faults she may have should be bred out, if this is possible, and this can only be done if you recognize the fault. If you have purchased your bitch

171

Dr and Mrs Graham Rogers' top-winning stud-dog in 1985, Sh.Ch. Chaigmarsh Sudden Impact, sired by Ch. Ardencote Alexander, himself top-winning stud-dog twice. Sudden Impact in turn was sire of Mompesson Dream Chaser who was top-winning stud-dog in 1991, 1993 and 1994.

from a reputable breeder, and you are not confident enough to make your own decision, then go back to the breeder of your bitch and ask his advice. Tell him which dogs you think you may like to use and ask which, if any, would be suitable. He will be only too happy to advise you, and will know which lines mix together well and which do not.

All of the early points mentioned regarding your bitch's suitability to be bred from apply equally to a stud-dog and should be considered.

The pedigrees of both dog and bitch should be put together and studied at length to see how they tie in with each other, if at all. The dog and bitch should be looked at carefully to see if they complement each other structurally. If one has a slight weakness or fault, be sure that the other does not have the same problem, otherwise you will be doubling up on it and will be likely to reproduce it.

If you own a dog who is to be used at stud, then he must be kept in peak condition at all times. As with a bitch, maximum fertility will come from a healthy, fit dog. Many people believe that a regular vitamin E supplement is beneficial to a stud dog and should be part of his diet, which should be sufficiently high in fat and protein content to keep him fit without getting fat. If it were that people gave you several weeks' notification of their intent to use your stud-dog you could build him up, ready for a bitch, but with bitches coming in season unexpectedly, and owners sometimes making their final decision to mate their bitch at the very last moment, it can be that very little notice is possible. It is therefore particularly important to keep your dog in peak condition at all times.

Remember, a great responsibility lies with you when you breed a litter, and be you the owner of the stud-dog or the bitch, or both, the puppies you produce will become an important part of the lives

Am. Ch. Chinoe's Adamant James, bred by Ann H. Roberts, seen here with judge Ann Clark and handler Clint Harris. 'D.J.' was a very influential sire in the USA during the 1970s (see Appendix II for pedigree).

of their new owners. As such, it is up to you to produce the best you possibly can, mentally and physically.

When to Mate Your Bitch

As mentioned earlier, it is generally considered best that an English Springer bitch does not have her first litter before her third season, which means that she is at least eighteen months of age. She will normally have two seasons a year, at six-monthly intervals, although this can vary slightly. A bitch should never be mated on consecutive seasons, and the Kennel Club will only register six litters from any one bitch.

It is polite to have selected the stud-dog you want to use well before your bitch comes in season, and to have agreed the stud fee with the owner of the dog.

One month before your bitch is due in season contact your vet and book her in for a booster injection. While you are there you can have her checked over to be sure that she is in perfect health, and collect some worm tablets. I normally worm my bitches before mating, and again when they are about half way through their pregnancy. I do not worm puppies or elderly dogs on the same day that they have a vaccination. I bath my bitches in an insecticidal shampoo about a week before mating, just to be sure that they are quite clean and free from parasites.

Usually, but not always, the bitch's vulva will start to swell slightly before her season actually starts, and this is worth watching for. She should be inspected daily around the time that she is due to come in season, and at the first sign of any blood the stud-dog owner should be contacted. This is 'day one' of her season, and a careful watch should be kept for changes in her from now on. Normally, bitches are ready to mate at around days ten, eleven, twelve, thirteen and fourteen, with the three middle days being the optimum time. This pattern can vary greatly, however, and I have had one bitch who was ready at day six and went off again very quickly. I had another who would have stood to be mated every day from seven to sixteen, and another, who caused me great concern, who was mated on her twenty-first day! Bitches are all very different but, generally speaking, when the discharge from the vulva changes from bright red to pink she is getting near, and when it goes clear with the vulva very swollen, she is ready. Another useful pointer can be if you gently scratch her back, at the base of the tail, her tail will normally turn to one side and she will present herself if she is ready. If you have trouble catching your bitch on the right day and do not manage to get her mated on this season, contact your vet before her next season as he can do some tests to tell you when she is ovulating.

The Mating

It is best not to feed your bitch on the day she is to be mated, until it is all over. If you have to travel a distance to the stud-dog, try to estimate when you are about half an hour away, and find a suitable spot to stop and give your bitch a walk and a chance to empty herself. I do not like to give travel pills to a bitch who is going to be mated, as I feel that they could have an effect on her, and I would rather have a mess in the car than a sleepy bitch who cannot respond as she should.

Different people handle their stud-dogs differently. Only once have I had to ask the owners of a bitch to 'please leave' while the mating took place, and that was not due to an embarrassed stud-dog but to a clingy bitch who would not leave 'mummy'. Should the stud-dog owner ask you to hand your bitch over and 'please leave the room' then his wishes should be respected. However, it would not be unreasonable to expect to see the dogs once they are tied, even if only from a distance.

I am a great believer in letting nature take its course, and whereas I do not put my stud-dogs at risk, I do like to let dog and bitch get acquainted in a confined area off the lead. Provided both dogs are wearing collars this has never caused me a problem and, after five minutes play, most bitches seem to stand quite happily once captured. This is not everyone's way though, and whatever approach the stud-dog owner takes, it should be respected. If, after half an hour of trying, the dog has not managed to penetrate the bitch then there may be something wrong. The bitch might not be ready, or may have gone over her time, or, if she is a maiden bitch it could be that she has an obstruction: a small ring of skin not far inside the vagina can sometimes cause this. There again, it could be that an inexperienced dog is over-keen and is missing the spot. If there is an obstruction, it is usually fairly simple to clear, and a quick trip to the vet's may well solve the problem, or at least tell you that this is where the problem lies.

175

After the introductory five minutes I like the owner of the bitch to hold her head while I hold the dog back. Once the dog is released he will mount the bitch and, hopefully, she will present herself to him. By 'present herself' I mean turn her tail to one side and lift her vulva, making it more easily accessible to the dog. If she does not do this it may mean that this is not the right day for her, but it could also mean that she is worried about what is happening to her, and is not responding as nature intended. This can be helped if the stud-dog owner supports the bitch from underneath, whilst kneeling by her side, being careful not to get in the way of the dog from this position. As the dog is thrusting to enter the bitch it is possible to push the bitch's vulva up to meet his penis. Some dogs do not mind being handled to help them in to the bitch, but I have never found this necessary.

Some bitches will react badly when the dog penetrates, and this is when the person holding her must be very vigilant. At any sign of snapping the lead should be wrapped round her foreface; a dog can easily be put off by a nip on the nose at this crucial point. Some stud-dog owners bind the bitch's foreface with a pop sock, or muzzle her, before trying for a mating, but I feel that this is likely to make her more difficult to mate.

Once inside the bitch, the dog's thrusting action will become much more intense, and he will almost skip from one back leg to the other with his enthusiasm. At this time his penis and two bulbs that form the base of his penis will be swelling inside the bitch, and this swelling will form the 'tie' which, in my experience, usually lasts about twenty minutes. If you look at your watch as the tie occurs you can be sure of this time factor. I have known a tie of as little as four minutes to be successful; I have heard of them lasting as long as an hour and a half, although I'm very glad to say that this has never happened to any of my dogs.

I feel that it is advisable to hold the dogs together in the mounted position for the first minute, and then, very gently, you can help the dog to 'turn' by easing one of his front legs off the bitch and then gently bringing the corresponding back leg over, so that they end up standing tail-to-tail. It is most important that you keep them as still as possible throughout all of this, as moving too much could damage both dog and bitch. Some bitches will throw themselves about and even try to roll over. It is very important that this is not allowed to happen. This is quite a stressful time for some bitches, and it is important to praise both bitch and dog and keep them calm.

When the tie is over take the bitch away from the dog and put her somewhere she can be quiet, probably back in the car. The dog should be taken back to his kennel or house and checked, to be sure that his penis has fully retracted back into the sheath. If it has not, a little cold water mixed with a touch of mild antiseptic, splashed on, usually does the trick. If it is left out it will become dry and swollen and painful.

Premature ejaculation can be a problem with some stud-dogs. This is where the dog ejaculates before he is inside the bitch: his penis and the two bulbs will come out fully, and it is normally down to an over-enthusiastic stud. This is not easy to deal with. The dog must be kept as quiet and as calm as possible, and if there is another dog available it is sometimes beneficial to tease the bitch with a different dog and then present her to the stud when she is totally ready to stand. Even then, if you do not get a direct hit at the first go it can be all over, and once the dog has ejaculated and is totally out of his sheath you will need to rest him for at least an hour and be sure that he is all back together properly before he can try again.

The Paperwork

Once a successful mating is achieved, the stud fee has to be paid and the paperwork sorted out. I normally give clients a stud receipt detailing the dog's name and stud fee paid, a copy of the dog's pedigree, and a signed Kennel Club registration form.

Reading a pedigree can be quite confusing if you are not familiar with the names and abbreviations. Ch. on the pedigree means that the dog is a Champion, which means that he has won three or more Challenge Certificates in the show ring and has gained his Show Gundog Working Certificate. Sh.Ch. on your pedigree means that the dog is a Show Champion and has won three or more Challenge Certificates in the show ring. F.T.Ch. means that the dog is a Field Trial Champion and has won a first at two different field trials in open stakes for Spaniels, or has won the Championship for Spaniels other than Cockers. These titles and the names of the dogs who hold them are normally highlighted in red on pedigrees.

It is normal for names on the pedigree to contain the affix of the breeder of the dog. If the affix comes before the dog's name, for example Ardencote Assurance, then that dog was bred by the holder of the affix Ardencote, unless it was that the holder of the affix

Mrs Ellen Dobson's Ch. Teesview Titus, a big winner in the ring and a very successful sire. (See Appendix II for pedigree: sire of Sh.Ch. Pandora of Truelindale.)

Ardencote bred both of the parents of the dog, in which case Ardencote can still be put first provided it is being used on a dog owned by the holder of the affix. Some dogs may have two affixes attached to their name, one before the name and one after the name: the affix before the name would be that of the owner of the dog, and the one after would be the affix of the new owner of the dog, unless someone had bought the dog, added their own affix, and then sold him on again, which does happen in some cases. Just to confuse the matter further, new owners do not always add their affix to puppies they have bought in. Therefore, just because a dog only has the affix of the breeder, it does not mean that he is still in the ownership of that breeder.

Mr and Mrs Doug Sheppard's Ch. Cliffhill Julius, a son of the influential sire Ch. Teesview Titus, who himself has left his mark on the breed in the UK and Scandinavia.

Line-Breeding

When you find the same names cropping up in your dog's pedigree more than once, back in the grandparents or great-grandparents, this is line-breeding. It involves mating related but not too closely related stock: a mating between great-uncle and great-niece, grandfather and granddaughter, or between dogs who share the same grandparents, are good examples. Line-breeding is quite a common practice amongst breeders who are trying to perpetuate a particularly good point, or points, of an ancestor. But it should be remembered that it is also possible for bad points to be doubled-up on, and that advice from experienced breeders who have had first-hand knowledge of those ancestors is very valuable.

Inbreeding

This is a much closer mating which could, for example, be a mother-to-son or brother-to-sister mating, and it should be undertaken only after great consideration, by a very experienced breeder who has an extensive knowledge of what is behind both the dog and bitch pedigrees, and with two animals who are considered to be of outstanding merit. The important thing to remember is that this can bring faults to the fore as well as good points. It can affect the temperament of the offspring, as well as possibly bring out health problems that have hitherto been hidden.

Outcrossing

This is when two unrelated dogs are mated to bring some fresh blood in to a line, possibly to try and eradicate a problem or obtain a desired attribute. When outcrossing, you should be very careful to select a dog who has all of the attributes you require and who has proved himself capable of passing them on to his offspring. This type of mating can often prove to be disappointing, bringing out the bad rather than the good points in both parents. However, should you be fortunate enough to get a pleasing puppy from this type of mating and then line-breed him back to your original line, it is generally believed that the result can be good.

Genetics

This is an extremely complicated subject, about which volumes have been written, and it is impossible to include here an in-depth study, which is in any case outside the scope of this book. However, it is important that the prospective breeder should at the very least understand the basic principles which govern genetic inheritance in dogs. I shall therefore endeavour to provide a simple outline.

Every dog has thirty-nine pairs of chromosomes. These chromosomes contain genes, which dictate the make-up of the dog. By make-up is implied not just the external physical characteristics that are visible, but also the characteristics that do not manifest themselves in visible ways. The genes are arranged in a specific order, occupying specific locations, within the chromosomes, and this order, or pattern, is repeated within corresponding chromosomes. The genes occupying corresponding locations in the chromosomes affect the same characteristic, though sometimes in different ways.

When the reproductive cells are formed, the pairs of chromosomes separate, so that each sperm or ovum contains only one of each pair of chromosomes. When a sperm fertilizes an ovum, the chromosome carrying genetic information from the male comes together with the corresponding chromosome from the female, thus forming a new pair of chromosomes in the offspring.

It is worth pointing out here that contrary to popular belief, an individual inherits all his genes from both parents, each parent contributing half. It is not possible for an individual to inherit all his genes from only one parent.

Dominant and Recessive Genes

Since the genetic make-up of one animal is inherited from two parents, whose genes may conflict, nature provides that each gene, and therefore the characteristic controlled by that gene, is either dominant or recessive. So, taking coat colour as a simplified example, black is always dominant to liver, which means that if an animal inherits the gene for a black coat from one parent and the gene for liver from the other parent, black will prevail: the animal's own coat colour will be black, even though it will also carry the gene for liver colouring. If that dog is then paired with another black-coated dog, who also carries the recessive gene for liver colouring, there is a fair chance that they will both pass on their recessive genes to one puppy, and amongst a litter produce a liver-coated dog, even though they themselves are both black.

So, a recessive gene characteristic will be outwardly apparent only if it has paired with another similar recessive gene: an animal with a liver-coloured coat will have inherited the recessive gene for liver colouring from *both* parents, regardless of the parents' own apparent coat colour. It is in this way that it is possible for two dogs to produce something in their puppy that is not actually visible in either of them.

In symbolic illustrations of the pairing of genes, the dominant gene is always indicated by a capital letter (in the following example, X); the recessive gene is indicated by the lower case of that letter (x). Unfortunately for breeders, the gene controlling Progressive Retinal Atrophy (PRA) – and, for that matter, many other inherited

181

diseases – is recessive. This means that a dog who is apparently free of the disease may yet be carrying it, and may therefore pass it on to his offspring. The following diagram gives the results of a test for the incidence of PRA in offspring produced from a test mating between a blind dog affected by PRA and a sighted bitch who nonetheless carries the recessive gene for PRA:

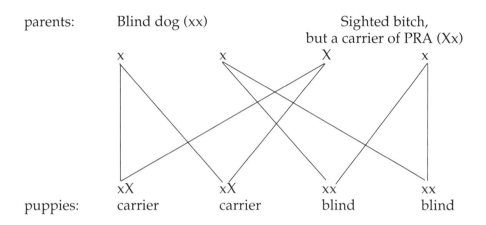

If the blind dog were mated to an unaffected bitch that was not a carrier, the likely results would be as follows:

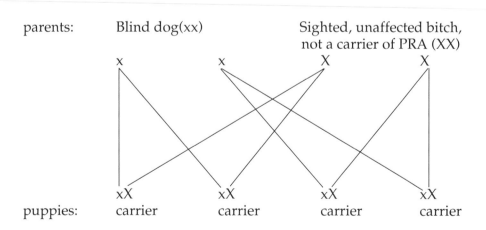

In this next example, two apparently normal dogs, which nonetheless both carry the recessive PRA gene, are mated:

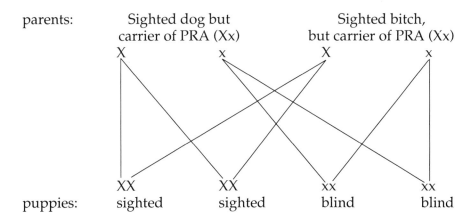

parents: Sighted dog but   Sighted bitch,
          carrier of PRA (Xx)   but carrier of PRA (Xx)

          XX   XX   xx   xx
puppies: sighted   sighted   blind   blind

It could be that the carriers in the second example are bred on from for several generations before the recessive genes from two carrier dogs unite again (as in the third example) to produce outwardly affected (blind) dogs; or it could happen in the next generation. So the main difficulty for breeders lies in trying to determine whether a dog possesses the recessive gene for a particular characteristic.

Whilst genetics is a very complex and specialist field in which there remains much research to be done, these simplified examples illustrate the basic principles when applied to the inheritance of one characteristic, in this case PRA. As such, they demonstrate the importance of knowing as much as possible about the backgrounds of the dogs from whom you are breeding. There is no disgrace in breeding a dog that is found to have a hereditary defect, as long as you learn from the mistake and do not repeat it.

Why Breed?

After all that has been written in this chapter, you now need to decide whether breeding a litter is really for you, why you are breeding this litter, and whether it really is in the best interests of the breed.

We, the breeders, have the future of our breed in our hands, and should take great care of it. In ten, twenty or thirty years' time, what we are doing with the breed today will still be having an effect. So before embarking on a breeding programme, you must genuinely feel that you can better the breed in the long term.

Your Kennel Club Affix

If you are going to breed a litter of puppies, presumably you will want your own affix registered with the Kennel Club. This process takes quite a long time and it would be advisable to apply to the Kennel Club for your affix about six months before you want to use it. You will need an application form from the Kennel Club and you will need to think of six different choices of words that you would like as your affix. Things to remember when picking these names are that they must not be the name of a place or a person; that once a word has been used as an affix, provided the owner of that affix is paying their annual maintenance fee, then that word, or any word that is considered too similar to it, may not be used by anyone else; and that the total number of letters in a dog's name, including the affix, should not exceed twenty-four. Therefore, the shorter your affix, the more letters you can use in the actual name. For example, my affix Ardencote has nine letters, which leaves me fifteen letters for the dog's name. Remember that when you breed a litter, your affix goes before the name. If you wish to add your affix to the name of a dog you have not bred, it goes after the name, unless you bred both parents of the dog when it goes before the name.

10

Pregnancy and Whelping

Be careful with your bitch after mating: she can still be attractive to other dogs, and could still possibly be mated for anything up to a week after you have had her mated to the dog of your choice.

Misalliance

Accidents will happen and, if an unwanted mating takes place, an injection from your vet within forty-eight hours will stop a pregnancy. It has, however, been suggested that this injection may affect future matings, so vigilance when your bitch is in season is strongly recommended.

Is She in Whelp?

The minute she is mated, you will be desperate to know whether she is in whelp. The earliest signs are the shape and size of her nipples and vulva. During her season, her vulva will have swollen considerably and usually, if a bitch is in whelp, it will not shrink back to its original size, but will stay a little swollen. With a bitch who is not in whelp, it will shrink back to its original size as usual. A bitch's nipples may also swell slightly when in season, although not always. It is quite likely that if her nipples are larger and more pert than usual when her season is over, she may be in whelp. Sometimes the nipples will also look quite pink. These things can also be signs that she is going to have an elaborate false pregnancy (see below) though, so are not foolproof ways to tell.

Some people are able to feel the puppies, like a little string of peas, inside the bitch from about three and a half weeks after conception, and can even tell you how many there are. I have tried and tried and simply cannot master this art.

Another way of being sure that your bitch is in whelp is to have her scanned. This can be done after week four of the pregnancy, and it will give you a definite answer as to whether your bitch is in whelp or not. However, I have found that it is not always very accurate on numbers of puppies inside.

False or Phantom Pregnancy

Some bitches are very prone to this problem, and can suffer with it right from their first season. Others will only have phantom pregnancies if they have been mated but failed to conceive. They will show many of the signs of being in whelp, often producing milk and mothering toys and sometimes other animals. There may be no need for treatment, but in bad cases I have found Pulsatilla 30 a useful remedy here, given three times a day. Obviously, if you are concerned about your bitch's health, then contact your vet.

Care of Your Bitch when In Whelp

Once your bitch has been mated, the temptation is to start to 'feed her up'. This is not necessary. The puppies will do very little growing for the first five weeks after conception and you will do more harm than good by over-feeding her and ending up with a fat bitch at whelping.

With modern foods, provided you use a product developed for use with in-whelp bitches you will not need to add any vitamins or minerals to her diet, although some people do like to give vitamin E which, it is believed, increases fertility. From about half way through your bitch's pregnancy you can start to increase her food very slightly until, by the time she whelps, she is getting about one-third more food than she was at conception. It may be that as the puppies grow within her she will find eating big meals uncomfortable, and you may like to split her meals down to two, or even three, a day. If you normally feed a dry complete food, or a dry biscuit with meat, I feel that it is better to soak the food, during the last two weeks of pregnancy, to help the bitch to digest it.

I am a great believer in homeopathy: my vet says that it cannot do any harm, and that if I am happy, it must be doing some sort of good! Throughout my bitches' pregnancies I like to give them one

PREGNANCY AND WHELPING

Feb	Dec	Jan	Nov	Dec	Oct	Nov	Sept	Oct	Aug	Sept	July	Aug	June	July	May	June	Apr	May	Mar	Apr	Feb	Mar	Jan
2	1	3	1	3	1	3	1	3	1	2	1	3	1	3	1	3	1	3	1	5	1	5	1
3	2	4	2	4	2	4	2	4	2	3	2	4	2	4	2	4	2	4	2	6	2	6	2
4	3	5	3	5	3	5	3	5	3	4	3	5	3	5	3	5	3	5	3	7	3	7	3
5	4	6	4	6	4	6	4	6	4	5	4	6	4	6	4	6	4	6	4	8	4	8	4
6	5	7	5	7	5	7	5	7	5	6	5	7	5	7	5	7	5	7	5	9	5	9	5
7	6	8	6	8	6	8	6	8	6	7	6	8	6	8	6	8	6	8	6	10	6	10	6
8	7	9	7	9	7	9	7	9	7	8	7	9	7	9	7	9	7	9	7	11	7	11	7
9	8	10	8	10	8	10	8	10	8	9	8	10	8	10	8	10	8	10	8	12	8	12	8
10	9	11	9	11	9	11	9	11	9	10	9	11	9	11	9	11	9	11	9	13	9	13	9
11	10	12	10	12	10	12	10	12	10	11	10	12	10	12	10	12	10	12	10	14	10	14	10
12	11	13	11	13	11	13	11	13	11	12	11	13	11	13	11	13	11	13	11	15	11	15	11
13	12	14	12	14	12	14	12	14	12	13	12	14	12	14	12	14	12	14	12	16	12	16	12
14	13	15	13	15	13	15	13	15	13	14	13	15	13	15	13	15	13	15	13	17	13	17	13
15	14	16	14	16	14	16	14	16	14	15	14	16	14	16	14	16	14	16	14	18	14	18	14
16	15	17	15	17	15	17	15	17	15	16	15	17	15	17	15	17	15	17	15	19	15	19	15
17	16	18	16	18	16	18	16	18	16	17	16	18	16	18	16	18	16	18	16	20	16	20	16
18	17	19	17	19	17	19	17	19	17	18	17	19	17	19	17	19	17	19	17	21	17	21	17
19	18	20	18	20	18	20	18	20	18	19	18	20	18	20	18	20	18	20	18	22	18	22	18
20	19	21	19	21	19	21	19	21	19	20	19	21	19	21	19	21	19	21	19	23	19	23	19
21	20	22	20	22	20	22	20	22	20	21	20	22	20	22	20	22	20	22	20	24	20	24	20
22	21	23	21	23	21	23	21	23	21	22	21	23	21	23	21	23	21	23	21	25	21	25	21
23	22	24	22	24	22	24	22	24	22	23	22	24	22	24	22	24	22	24	22	26	22	26	22
24	23	25	23	25	23	25	23	25	23	24	23	25	23	25	23	25	23	25	23	27	23	27	23
25	24	26	24	26	24	26	24	26	24	25	24	26	24	26	24	26	24	26	24	28	24	28	24
26	25	27	25	27	25	27	25	27	25	26	25	27	25	27	25	27	25	27	25	29	25	29	25
27	26	28	26	28	26	28	26	28	26	27	26	28	26	28	26	28	26	28	26	30	26	30	26
28	27	29	27	29	27	29	27	29	27	28	27	29	27	29	27	29	27	29	27			31	27
		30	28	30	28	30	28	30	28	29	28	30	28	30	28	30	28	30	28				
		31	29	31	29			31	29	30	29	31	29	31	29			31	29				
Mar 1	28	Feb 1	30	Jan 1	30	Dec 1	29	Nov 1	30	Oct 1	30	Sept 1	30	Aug 1	30	July 1	29	June 1	30	May 1	27	Apr 1	28
2	29			2	31	2	30	2	31	2	31			2	31	2	30	2	31	2	28	2	29
3	30																					3	30
4	31																					4	31

Gestation table. First column lists mating date; second column lists whelping date.

tablet of Caulophyllum strength 30 once a week. The tablet should be crushed between two clean spoons and tipped onto the tongue. It should not come into contact with your hands or anything else, and should be given at least half an hour away from food. Since I have been using this, my bitches have not had any problems whelping at all, and so I do believe that it works well. I know of other people who believe in giving raspberry leaf tablets throughout pregnancy, as this is also said to make for easy whelping. There is no scientific proof for either, but they do seem to help.

Three weeks before my bitches are due to whelp I like to worm them. Some people's worm control programme involves using a small dose of a certain type of wormer every day throughout the entire pregnancy. I think it would be difficult to remember to do this every day, and have not had any bad worm problems using my method of worming them before they come in season, or just as they come in, and then treating them again, three weeks prior to whelping.

Sometimes throughout pregnancy a bitch will have a slight discharge. I have never found this to be a cause for worry, provided it is not dark-coloured or smelly.

Your bitch should continue with her normal exercise throughout her pregnancy for as long as she is happy to. A fit, not fat, bitch will have an easier time whelping.

The Last Two Weeks Before Whelping

At this time I like to trim some of the feather off my bitches, how much obviously being dependent on whether I want to show them soon after the puppies are born or not. I have found that if I do not trim it down now, the puppies seem to drag it out, which can often take longer to get back. The tips of the ears tend to get in a mess if they are left too long with mum cleaning up after the puppies. I also like to give the bitch a bath in a mild ordinary shampoo, making quite sure that the nipples and surrounding area are clean.

I will now move her to her whelping bed to give her time to get accustomed to her surroundings. The whelping bed must be big enough for the bitch to be able to stretch out in it, with room to allow for the rapid growth of the puppies. It is better for it to be too big than too small. It would be a very poor mother who would let her puppy get left out on his own to get cold, but it is quite easy for a puppy to get laid on in too confined an area. The bed I use for

The whelping bed.

Springer bitches measures 3ft by 4ft (90cm by 1.2m), with a whelping rail 4in (10cm) in and 5in (12cm) up; this goes all the way round the walls and prevents puppies being squashed. The bedding should be stiff, I use a piece of fairly new fleecy bed and put newspaper underneath it to soak up the wet that goes through. The design of these newer beddings is excellent, some allow wet to pass one way and prevent it from coming back. It is important that the bedding is not too soft, however, or your bitch may inadvertently scratch it up and bury a puppy.

My bitches all whelp inside the house, but wherever you choose to whelp your bitch, the bed will need scrubbing out and disinfecting and a piece of clean, disinfected bedding should be put in it. If you do not want to use a whelping bed, but prefer your bitch to whelp outside in a straw bed, then this must be prepared early and the bed and straw must be disinfected. The bitch will flatten the straw down to make a nest. After a few days, fresh straw can be added to this for her to flatten down further. This way the bed will end up deep and flattened. If you put your bitch into a fresh bed just before whelping the straw would be too loose and the puppies would tend to get lost in it and, as the bitch made her bed she would

189

soon be down to the base. It is also worth remembering that if she is going to whelp outside on straw, it is better to have a wooden base underneath her rather than concrete, as wood will feel warmer.

Some people send their bitches away to whelp. If you are planning to do this then I would advise sending her three weeks before she is due. Not only will this enable her to get used to her surroundings but it will also enable her to build up the antibodies needed for those surroundings to safeguard her puppies against infection.

Wherever you are planning to whelp your bitch, she should have her own space with some privacy.

There is a train of thought now that says infra-red lights are damaging to the puppies' eyes, and many people have consequently gone over to using white heat lamps, should extra heating be necessary. All of these things need considering and organizing before your bitch is due.

Oddities During Pregnancy

Some bitches will go off their food in the third or fourth week of pregnancy, almost as though they have the equivalent to morning sickness. If this happens to your bitch do not worry unduly: as long as she seems quite happy and fit there should be no need for concern, and she will probably be back on full diet and asking for more within three or four days. Often, when in whelp, a bitch becomes very sloppy and affectionate, demanding far more attention than she normally would, and sometimes she will look for other animals to mother: the cat is a favourite substitute puppy in our house. Sometimes, during the last week of pregnancy, a bitch may be sick after eating her food. Left to her own devices she will normally eat it up again and manage to keep it down the second time. Another oddity I once experienced before whelping was when a previously clean bitch started making lots of little messes about the place. She was perfectly well and happy, and would go out to do her main business but would not, or could not, stop doing these little piles. After great discussion on the subject it was decided that either she had a huge litter pushing on her internally, or, as her puppies were pushing out their waste, so it was passing straight through her.

Countdown to Whelping

Some bitches will go right to the day of whelping without any fuss whatsoever; others like to make a tremendous fuss for anything up to three days before they actually whelp! My very first Springer was one of the latter, and by the time she whelped I was quite exhausted through lack of sleep and was a nervous wreck.

Usually, three or four days before whelping, you will notice a difference in the shape of your bitch, particularly in the quarters, and it may be that she is not moving as soundly behind as previously she did.

Some people keep a check on the bitch's temperature, and when it drops to 98°F (36.6°C) it is generally expected that she will whelp within the next twenty-four to forty-eight hours. I have not found this a very reliable method of monitoring my bitches, and I find that they do not much enjoy me attacking them with a thermometer every few hours!

Some bitches will go off their food before whelping. Most will make beds, hopefully in their own beds. This is a time when they do need watching closely as it is quite common, particularly in a maiden bitch, for them to look for their own spot, perhaps under the garden shed or under the biggest holly bush in the garden. Getting them back in to the clean surroundings that you have so carefully prepared for them can be quite tricky, particularly if their water happens to break whilst they are out.

This behaviour may go on for days, or it may hardly be noticed to have happened, so do not panic as soon as your bitch starts bed-making and imagine puppies must be on the way: if you panic she will sense it, and you will both end up in a state.

Equipment to Have Ready Just In Case

A small bottle and teat, usually available from the vet's. Dried Puppy milk. Electrolyte, of the type used for babies, and available from good chemists. A hot-water bottle. A sturdy cardboard box with some old towels or a blanket in the bottom. Three clean, dry towels. A bottle of Rescue Remedy, available from good health shops. A spray of suitable disinfectant which you can obtain from your vet.

Whelping

Once the bitch's water goes, whelping proper is under way. I find it rare to see this magic water go, and tend to look for the signs of contractions as an indication that the bitch has 'started'.

Often, before contractions proper start, the bitch will become restless, will pant a lot and will do her best to ruck up the very nice bed that you have so carefully made for her. I am sorry to say that this can go on for up to twenty-four hours without the contractions actually starting, and it is a very stressful time, both for the owner and the bitch. If she has been at this stage for more than twenty-four hours, for your peace of mind, it would be as well to contact your vet.

I have been very fortunate over the last few years and my bitches have taken to whelping during the day. This is quite unusual, as it is normal for them to whelp in the middle of the night. I would therefore advise leaving a light on all the time in the room where the bitch is to whelp. The very act of turning the light on when you come in to check her, and then turning it off again when you leave, can be disturbing for the bitch. Also, have a torch to hand so that if your bitch wants to go outside to empty herself, you can go with her and check that she does not drop a puppy in the dark.

Early Labour

Before the bitch actually starts to have contractions, she will often appear to be shivering, or quivering down her back. It should not be long after this, perhaps an hour or two, that the first contractions will be seen and you may see the water bag appear. Many people are amazed at the amount of fluid that seems to come from this bag. It is nothing to worry about, and can be useful in a breed such as ours, as it often wets the feather sufficiently to make us realize that the water has, in fact, broken. Another signal that labour is under way is the sweet, musty smell that comes from the bitch's water. It will probably not wet the bedding as much as you would expect, as the bitch will lick it up rapidly; this helps induce labour. A bitch's temperature will fluctuate before whelping and at some stage in the two days prior to whelping it will drop from the normal 100–100.5°F (37.7–38°C) to about 98°F (36.6°C). This drop, however, may only be transient and is no clear sign of how soon your bitch will whelp. Personally I do not consider it worth stressing the bitch by constantly

192

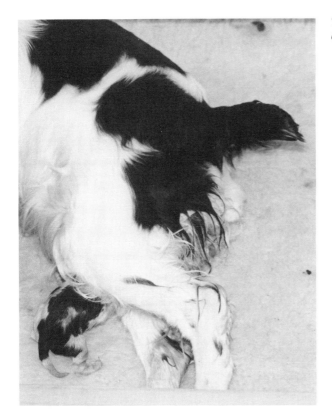

The tail raised with contraction.

taking her temperature for the small indication that it may give you of when she will whelp.

I find that once the contractions have started in earnest, that is, the quivering down the spine has ceased and the bitch is actually seen to be pushing at regular intervals, the first puppy will appear within twenty minutes to half an hour. If the bitch goes longer than two hours between the water and the first puppy, or between puppies without appearing to be trying very hard to have them, or for more than one hour of pushing hard with no puppy showing, then contact your vet and take his advice.

As the contractions become stronger and more regular, the bitch's tail will rise as she pushes, and you should soon see the first of the puppies. In a normal delivery, all you will see at this stage is the edge of the water bag at the mouth of the vulva. Do not be tempted to try and help it out at this stage: just let the bitch get on with it and, if she is looking to you instead of getting on with her job, try

193

to get yourself a vantage point where she will not notice you. It is very difficult, with some bitches, to know what to do for the best when they are looking to you for help. I have found that if you can let nature take its course, without putting the puppies' lives at risk by not being on hand when you are needed, then this is best; but some bitches will only settle if you are 'holding their hand'. Only you will know if this is the case, and will have to make that judgement for yourself.

The Birth

Provided your bitch continues to push, the first puppy should gradually emerge, in the bag, during the next ten to fifteen minutes. Should it take a little longer, do not worry unduly as long as your bitch is continuing with contractions and is not distressed.

As the first puppy is born the bitch may give out a yelp. This is not uncommon and is nothing to worry about. The next stage is when I often find I am needed: some bitches are very diligent and will tear the bag and start licking the first puppy the minute he emerges; others are not so thorough, and it may be necessary for you to break the bag and clear the puppy's mouth of mucus. This is a slimy job, but the puppy must not be left lying there in the sack for too long, or he will drown. As you break the sack and clear his mouth he may already be spluttering and choking a little, and speed is of the essence. Break the sack, clear the mouth, and if the umbilical cord is still attached to the afterbirth then very carefully, using both hands, break this with your nails about one and a half inches away from the puppy's tummy, being sure not to put any pressure on the end of the cord that is attached to the puppy. I find that by tearing it in this way you are having the same effect as the bitch chewing it off and it will not bleed, which it may do if cut with scissors. If your bitch is happy to do all of this for herself then do let her, but be ready to take over if she is not. Once the puppy is free from the bag take one of the clean towels and rub him from the tail forward. This action will simulate the mother's licking and, by going from back to front, will help clear any fluid that may be in his lungs.

The bitch will normally eat the sack and the afterbirth: not a pretty sight, but nature knows best; and this will sustain her for efforts to come, as well as acting to stimulate the natural contractions.

The bitch should lick the puppy as soon as possible after the birth,

The head is out.

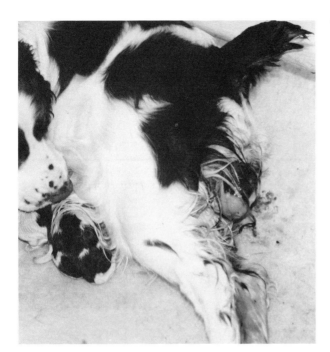

The puppy arrives out of the sack.

not only to clean him but also to form the maternal bond and encourage the puppy to suckle. It may be that she seems more interested in licking the bedding where the fluid from the sack has gone. This is quite normal and it is best just to put the puppy where she is licking. Normally, she will then transfer her attention from bedding to puppy.

The puppy should be suckling within five minutes of birth, but again, do not worry or be tempted to interfere. Try to let nature take its course. Provided the puppy is healthy it is amazing how quickly he will find the nipples.

More Puppies

A single whelp is unusual, and it is most likely that more puppies will follow. It can be that one will follow another very quickly and the bitch will need help, if this is the case, to get them dry and comfortable. I am reluctant to take puppies away from a bitch at birth but if she has a very large litter then it is sometimes necessary. Should this be the case, fill a hot-water bottle and wrap it up well in an old blanket or towel. Put this inside the strong cardboard box and once a puppy has had a good tummy full of milk, transfer him to the box. Unless the bitch is ill I find that this is the only satisfactory way to take whelps away from the bitch without her getting distressed and without them suffering through a lack of that vital first milk. By taking puppies away and putting them in a box in this way the bitch will always have whelps suckling, and the chances are that she will not notice that any have gone. If she does notice and is distressed, then put them back.

It may well be necessary to move puppies around a little in the box, to avoid the bitch sitting on them or dropping another puppy on them, but do try not to handle them too much.

As previously mentioned, the gap between puppies should never be left for longer than two hours without consulting your vet. Sometimes the bitch simply gets tired between puppies and settles down for a little snooze; this is quite common and often happens about halfway through the whelping. It will usually only last for twenty minutes or half an hour, and then she will wake up refreshed and get on with the job in hand.

If my bitches have gone two and a half or three hours and are still whelping, I give them about half a pint of warm milk, diluted slightly with water, with a good tablespoon of glucose in it. For the twenty-four hours immediately associated with whelping the bitch will probably not be able to cope with anything solid, and this milk mixture, given three or four times, will help keep her strength up.

I normally keep a note of time and sex of each puppy born. Some people weigh them, but I feel that this is not necessary at a time when as little interference as possible is best. The time lapse between puppies is interesting to keep for future reference, and can be useful information for the vet, should he be needed.

Is it All Over?

As each puppy is born, so each placenta should be accounted for. This is not always easy but it is best to know that the bitch has not retained one as it could cause complications in a few days' time.

It is difficult to judge whether the bitch has finished whelping. You will have noticed as whelping has been in progress that it is possible to see the puppies' shapes inside the bitch, moving into the birth canal. However, it can be that the last puppy is in the birth canal or is still hidden up in the rib cage. When this is the case it is very easy to think that the bitch has finished, because you can feel nothing, and then another puppy appears quite unexpectedly. If you are at all concerned it is probably advisable to have your vet check the bitch over after you think she has finished. Unfortunately, not all vets are willing to make house calls for this purpose and I would not consider taking a bitch of mine, with or without her puppies, into a surgery where she has the risk of picking up infection, nor subject her to the stress of the journey.

Complications

What is described above is an outline of a normal whelping. All bitches and all whelpings will vary slightly and I hope that this will be helpful. I will now run through some of the complications that can be found in whelping, with a few simple remedies, and with the hope that it will give you an idea of how to tell when things are going wrong.

Breech Birth

Normally a puppy is born head first in the sack, as previously

197

described, although it can be that the sack breaks as the puppy comes out. The puppy may come out hind feet first: this is often called a breech birth, although it is only a true breech if the back legs are flexed at the hips. A true breech can well cause problems, whereas a rear presentation, with the hind feet and tail coming first together, is quite common and rarely causes any trouble. If it is obvious that the bitch cannot push the puppy out, it is quite possible that you have a true breech, or that the puppy is presented with his head turned to one side. In both cases it will be very difficult for the bitch to move the puppy, and it is advisable to call for veterinary help if it is obvious that she is having a problem moving the puppy down the birth canal.

Inertia

This is the term used when a bitch opens up, ready to whelp, but simply does not start contractions, or stops some time during whelping and does not start again, although there are more puppies inside. I had one bitch who would give up between each puppy and, as this was in the days before I discovered Caulophyllum, the vet used to have to give her an injection of Oxytocin to make her start to push again. Since I have been using Caulophyllum, this has not been necessary and most of my bitches have whelped very easily and quickly. If, however, I have had one who has slowed down or given up, a small dose of Caulophyllum 30 every fifteen minutes, for up to four doses, has always seemed to work, often by the second dose.

Retaining the Placenta

Sometimes a puppy will be born having already come out of its bag, and the placenta will be retained inside the bitch. I have had cases where up to four placentas have been retained, as the puppies have been born without them. It is difficult to be sure that all have been passed, as bitches often eat them very quickly and make it difficult to count them. If I am in any doubt as to whether all placentas have been accounted for I give Secale 6, at a rate of one tablet every hour, for three hours. If you are at all worried, then a telephone call to your vet is advisable.

Sometimes a puppy will be born out of the bag but still attached by the umbilical cord to the placenta, which is still inside the bitch.

Do be careful in this case not to pull on the puppy and risk ruptur-ing its stomach where the cord is attached. If the placenta will not easily follow the puppy out of the bitch, then get as long a piece of umbilical cord as you can and sever it using your nails, as described previously. Hopefully, the placenta will come away from the bitch as she is pushing with the next puppy.

Umbilical Hernia

It would seem that if a puppy has had too much strain put on his umbilical cord during or shortly after birth, it can cause a small umbilical hernia, which will show as a fleshy lump on the stomach when the puppy is grown. This condition can also be a hereditary fault, which some vets believe should not be perpetuated. I have, however, had one or two bitches over the years with this oddity and never found it to be detrimental to them in any way.

Weak and Drowning Puppies

Some puppies are born very waterlogged, and I find that you have got to be rough to be kind in this situation: you can almost imagine that you are squeezing the fluid from the puppy, and that is just what you need to do. If rubbing vigorously from the tail towards the head does not work, then try squeezing with the towel as you rub from the tail towards the head. If this still does not seem to be sufficient, then I have had great success treating the puppy as I would a lamb with similar problems, and have literally swung him from side to side as roughly as I dare, by the back legs. This seems very extreme but it is essential that you clear his lungs as quickly and as completely as possible, and it is better to be a little rough than to lose the puppy. I am very happy to say that I have never lost a puppy in these conditions, but have often been very con-cerned when trying to get the fluid from his lungs.

The other problem that calls for drastic measures is when a puppy appears dead at birth. I do not mean actually decomposing and obviously very dead, but just totally lacking in outward signs of life. The first thing I do under these circumstances is to take the puppy between my hands in a towel and rub him like mad. After about thirty seconds of doing this I then give the puppy a small dose of Rescue Remedy, another thing available from good health shops and very good for shock in all types of animal. I then continue to rub very roughly. The puppy should not be cold, as he has presumably just been born. If he had been born while I was absent, and had become cold, I would lie him on a covered hot-water bottle while I rubbed. I continue to rub very roughly for about two minutes. If, by this time, I am getting no response I swing him, as for congested lungs, then I rub again for thirty seconds before giving another dose of Rescue Remedy, and more rubbing. If, after five minutes there is no response, I go for more drastic measures and actually clap the puppy between my hands in the towel for about ten claps, and follow that with more rubbing. If, after ten minutes there is still no response, all is probably lost. I am very fortunate I have never got to the last stage, but do remember, if you do nothing the puppy has no chance; you do not have time to call your vet, so anything you can do has to be worth trying, even if it seems very rough.

Difficulty in Suckling

The first thing you should check, if a puppy seems to be having difficulty suckling, is whether he has a cleft palate. It is simple to use your finger to feel the roof of his mouth. If you are unsure of what it should feel like, then check one or two other puppies for a comparison. If you do have a puppy with a cleft palate, consult your vet for further advice.

Most puppies will suckle by themselves within five or ten minutes of birth. I would not advise worrying puppy or bitch by trying to help what looks like a normal healthy puppy, until you have given him ten minutes to try for himself. If, after this time, he has still not managed to latch on to a teat, then place him very gently in front of the teat and ease a little milk from the teat onto the puppy's nose to give him the idea of what is there. If the puppy is trying to get onto the teat but is overshooting the mark, I find the best thing to do is to place my hand above the teat, so that without handling the puppy I am channelling him in the correct direction and stopping him overshooting the teat. With plenty of patience this method normally works. If not, then you can try opening the puppy's mouth very gently and, with your hand over the top of his head, your thumb on one side of his mouth and your forefinger on the other, place his lips over a teat from which you have already expressed a little milk using your other hand. This all takes time and tremendous patience, and it is most important to be very gentle with the puppy and reassuring with the bitch.

If the puppy is exhausted from a difficult birth and simply does not have the strength to suck, make up a glucose solution as follows: mix one level teaspoon of glucose powder with 30ml of cooled, boiled water. I also add one drop of Rescue Remedy to this. Glucose is easily absorbed directly through the roof of the mouth, so dip your finger in the solution and then touch it on the roof of the mouth and the front of the tongue. This should be continued very gently for five or ten minutes, and should be repeated every twenty minutes until the puppy picks up sufficiently to suck. You will be able to feel the suck reflex on your finger. If he has not picked up sufficiently to suck, do not be tempted to bottle-feed him milk until his rectal temperature is above 94°F (34.4°C), as any milk given when the puppy's temperature is less than this will stagnate in his stomach, adding to his problems. This is when an electrolyte solution should be fed. If you have been unable to obtain this, you can make your own using 1 pint of boiled, cooled water, 2½ teaspoons of glucose powder, ¼ teaspoon of salt and a pinch of bicarbonate of soda. This is not as good as the product you can purchase from vets and chemists but it will do to tide you over. If the suck reflex is not present the puppy will need tube-feeding. This should be undertaken with great care, and you would be best advised to speak to your vet before trying to feed a puppy by this method.

The Importance of the First Milk – Colostrum

Colostrum is the first milk that comes from the bitch. It is more creamy in colour and consistency than the milk produced later, and contains antibodies needed to protect the puppy. The puppy is most able to absorb these antibodies during the first eight hours of life, and the ability to absorb them ceases completely at about twenty-four hours of age. It is most important, therefore, that the puppy has this colostrum. If he is not well enough to take milk at this vital time, then it must be remembered that he will not have the protection of these antibodies.

Bitch Not Letting Down her Milk

Some maiden or nervous bitches do not let their milk down as quickly as they should after whelping. This can be very worrying, especially as we know that the colostrum is so essential for the puppy in those first few hours. Gently stimulating the teats can help

201

with this problem, and I give Urtica 30 at a rate of one dose every fifteen minutes for four doses, which has always seemed successful. If you are worried, then do consult your veterinary surgeon, who will probably give the bitch an injection of Oxytocin, which contains the necessary hormone not only to encourage a bitch to contract when whelping, but also to let her milk drop. This is not a common problem and, generally speaking, nature will take its course.

Mastitis

This is another uncommon problem which can in fact be the cause of a bitch not having sufficient milk available for her puppies. If it occurs, it is usually because a bitch has lost all or some of her litter, and is not at all common in a bitch rearing her full litter. If a bitch does lose all or some of her litter, then obviously nature has provided more milk than is needed, and I tend to dose the bitch with Urtica Urens 3. For a reduced litter I give one tablet every four hours for three doses and no more; for a bitch who has lost her whole litter, I give one tablet every hour for two days, and then one tablet four times daily for a further three or four days, dependent on how the milk situation looks.

If the teats are very sore and the bitch is not happy to let her puppies suckle, then hot flannels placed over the udder can ease the situation, and it may be necessary to milk her out by hand to remove the infected milk. Your vet's advice should be taken and he will probably advise antibiotics.

Eclampsia

Provided your bitch has been fed on a properly balanced diet throughout her pregnancy, she should have been able to supply all of the nutritional needs for the puppies. Once they are born, however, great demand is put on her. This is when I like to give my bitches calcium with vitamin D twice daily, to replace what is being taken from her already depleted resources. If the bitch's calcium level becomes too low, then she is likely to get Eclampsia, which can be fatal if not treated quickly. The symptoms are different to any others encountered after whelping, although they could be confused with those of a stressed bitch before whelping. The bitch will normally pant and be very restless; she may seem disorientated and stagger as she moves. It is *essential* to contact your veterinary surgeon *immediately* whether day or night and he will give her a large injection of calcium straight into her bloodstream. I cannot stress strongly enough that this is not a problem that can be left, and veterinary advice must be sought as soon as Eclampsia is suspected.

Deformed Puppies

I am a great believer in letting nature take its course, and should it be that you get an obviously deformed puppy, or one that the bitch consistently rejects, then the chances are that the kindest thing to do is to call out your vet and let him deal with the problem. If a bitch rejects a puppy, it is normally the maternal instinct judging the situation: on the three occasions that I have thought the bitch to be wrong, it has become quite apparent by three or four days of age that she knew better than I. One should always remember that at this very early age puppies will suffer very little, whereas if we succeed in rearing a deformed puppy then we have the responsibility of finding him a suitable caring home, where he and his owners will have to cope with his disability for the rest of his life.

Hand-Rearing Puppies

It is to be hoped that you will never have to hand-rear any puppies as it is an exacting and very time-consuming task since the puppies can do nothing for themselves. However, in the event that it becomes necessary the following guide-lines will be useful.

It is advisable to have a feeder bottle and teats in the medicine cupboard in case of emergency; they should be designed for use with animals rather than human babies (I bought mine from my vet). As colostrum is so important for the puppy to have a good start in life, it is a great advantage if the puppies have taken some from their dam. If not, it is useful to have some in the freezer, preferably taken from a bitch that lives in the same home as the puppies so that the colostrum will have antibodies to suit that area. After the puppy has taken some colostrum, it can gradually be replaced with one of the puppy milk substitutes that are obtainable for the purpose, providing that the puppy is healthy and has a normal temperature: approximately 95.3°F (36°C) at birth rising to 95.7°F (37°C) by one to two weeks, and up to 100°F (37.8°C) by four weeks.

Puppies will need feeding every two hours day and night, and an average Springer puppy will need approximately 10ml of milk per feed. After two weeks the quantities and intervals between feeds can gradually be increased. Do remember that the feeding equipment will need sterilizing just as it would for a human baby. An extremely important part of hand-rearing is to simulate the dam's licking of the puppies' abdomen and genitals, which is carried out not only for the purposes of keeping the puppies clean, but to stimulate the bowels and bladder. Without this stimulation, the puppies cannot defecate or urinate. It is therefore necessary to simulate the dam's actions after every feed: this is best done using cotton wool dampened with warm water and stroking the area around the genitals.

Solids can be introduced gradually as they would if the puppies were being reared by their dam, provided of course that they are healthy. Once they are well on to solids remember that milk will no longer be necessary and that they should be happily drinking water.

It is easy to imagine that the puppies will be best all kept together for warmth and comfort but they should be watched very carefully to see that they are not sucking each other. If this happens, they should be separated, each being housed in a box that is easy to keep clean such as a plastic stacker box. The puppies can be given a soft washable toy to cuddle up to if they have to live alone, although such a toy should not be of the sort that may shed loose hair.

For the first two weeks of life, orphan puppies should live at a constant temperature of 86°F (30°C); for the third week this can be allowed to drop gradually to 80°F (26.5°C); for the fourth week 70°F–75°F (22°C–24°C); and from the fifth week onwards, 70°F (22°C).

Postnatal Care of the Bitch

Your bitch has now produced her litter for you, and will rely on you to fulfil all her needs as the puppies grow and demands on her become greater. The need for extra calcium has already been mentioned and is most important, as is a good diet. Her energy requirement will have risen little throughout her pregnancy, compared to the demands placed on her now. All of the pet food manufacturers now have foods on the market for all of your dog's requirements and you should be able to ensure that your bitch gets all that she needs to maintain her own condition while giving the puppies what they need.

Daily checks on your bitch should be made to make sure she is well. There may be a slight discharge from the vulva. This is quite normal and, unless it becomes very smelly and a strange dark-green colour, should not cause any problems. Her teats should be checked regularly to be sure that there is no discomfort and that they are all working correctly.

She may be reluctant to leave the puppies at first, and you may find it necessary to put her on a lead to get her to go outside to empty herself. Try not to stress her but do encourage her to go out if at all possible. She will be far more comfortable if she empties herself, and a little walk will not only do her good but you will be able to see that she is functioning normally.

If the bitch gets diarrhoea it may be that this has been caused by eating too much afterbirth, or it may be that the puppies are finding her milk very rich, and in fact she has diarrhoea because she is cleaning up their mess. A good bitch will keep her puppies so clean that it may not be easy to notice that they have a problem. If the first cause seems likely, then treating the bitch alone will work; should it be the second cause, then you will need to treat the bitch and her puppies. Diarrhoea can be very debilitating and should not be left untreated. A phone call to your vet for advice would be best. I would try Arsen Alb 6, giving one tablet to the bitch every fifteen minutes for four tablets, and then one tablet four times a day for twenty-four hours. If this did not work I would then continue to dose the bitch four times a day and would also crush a tablet between two clean spoons and put a little onto the tongue of each puppy four times in the first hour, and then four times a day. I had one litter who were fine as long as I kept them on this but, as soon as I stopped, the diarrhoea started again. They had to remain on it for as long as they were suckling, and as soon as they were weaned the diarrhoea stopped.

After whelping, the bitch has to close up internally, and I have known bitches who, on the third or fourth day after whelping, would start making beds again. This can last for two or three days, and needs watching as they can become quite restless and bury their puppies in the bedding. I have put this down to the internal contractions being similar to the whelping contractions and causing a similar response.

Postnatal Care of the Whelps

Healthy puppies are quiet during the first couple of weeks of their lives and sleep a great deal of the time. All they require from life is a warm, comfortable bed and their mum. The bitch not only provides their single source of food but, by licking them, stimulates them to pass urine and faeces. A healthy puppy will normally double his birth weight by the first seven to ten days of life, and even a puppy born scraggy should be filled out and healthy-looking after the first twenty-four hours.

The newborn puppies' toe-nails grow with amazing speed and should be checked regularly and kept trimmed back, to avoid making the bitch's teats sore.

At three or four days of age the puppies should have their dew-claws removed. Personally, I like to remove hind and front dew-claws as I can see no reason for keeping the front ones, and the hind ones become very large and awkward if left. This is the time when tails should also be docked if you are planning to have them done. There is a world-wide differing of opinion on this subject at this time but in the UK, it is illegal for the layman to dock tails. The operation must be performed by a qualified veterinary practitioner.

At between ten days and two weeks the puppies' eyes will open and gradually, over the next week, will start to focus. At this time the puppies will find bright lights unpleasant, and these should be avoided. It will probably be several months before they have full vision. At two weeks puppies begin orientating towards sound, and by seventeen days the ears are normally fully open. Around this time they will start to walk about the box, and care should be taken that they are not getting too heavy for their little legs to support them. By eighteen days the puppies will be able to excrete without stimulation. At three weeks hearing should be very acute and if any puppy does not seem to be hearing properly by six weeks then he should be checked out.

Worming

I like to worm puppies at three weeks of age, then again at five weeks, and again just before they go to their new homes at seven weeks. I always get wormer from my vet and take his advice on what brand is best at the time. I worm the bitch at the same time as the puppies.

Weaning

During the first two or three weeks of the puppies' lives their mother will see to all of their needs and, dependent on the size of the litter and condition of the bitch, I would normally start weaning my puppies at about three weeks. Provided the bitch or puppies obviously do not need help sooner I like to start weaning two days after the puppies have had their first wormer at three weeks. I start them off on a good-quality tinned puppy food especially formulated for weaning puppies, as this is soft and easily digestible and contains vitamins and minerals that are necessary for their healthy development. I used to start my puppies on scraped beef and I know that many people still use this method, but I will take you through what I have found to be best.

On the first day I give them about a dessertspoonful each, just in one feed. On day two I give them the same quantity in two feeds, on day three the same in three feeds, and on day four the same in four feeds. Provided they are taking this happily and with no ill effects, I gradually increase the quantity over the next few days until they seem to be eating their fill in about five minutes. By this time they will probably have discovered the bitch's water bowl and they should be able to reach into it easily without risk of falling in.

At the start of week two I soak a little complete dry puppy food and mix this with the tinned meat. I give them more tinned meat than complete on day one, and gradually change it until they are of equal quantities. At this stage we should be at about four and a half weeks and, provided she is still well, the bitch will still be with her puppies for most of the time, coming away from them at feed times and for a bit of a rest. By now, if at all possible, I like to have the puppies and bitch housed somewhere that has the facility for the bitch to get away from the puppies when she feels inclined. If it is possible for the puppies to stay in the hustle and bustle of the house then I do feel that this is beneficial to their social development. However, if this is not practical and they have to be kennelled, the kennel should obviously be warm and dry. It is also a good idea to have a radio playing to get them used to noise.

By five weeks, I increase their feeds to five a day, and the bitch only goes in to them at night. After three days of this I take the bitch away altogether. After this gradual process of weaning, the bitch should not have too much milk to dry up and the puppies should be quite happy without her.

It still seems strange to me to wean puppies without giving them any milk in their diet, but I am assured by the pet food company and by my vet that it is not necessary as the modern foods are completely balanced to supply all of the growing puppies' requirements, and in fact if milk is introduced it will often upset their stomachs.

Teeth

The first teeth to come through will be the canines. These will start to show themselves at three weeks of age, and will be followed by the incisors, starting with the ones nearest the front and gradually working back. All of the puppies' first teeth should be through by the time they are eight weeks of age. The molars will not come through until the permanent teeth come to replace the milk teeth. By the time a puppy is ready to go to his new home it should be possible to see that his teeth are correctly positioned in his mouth. This is no guarantee that the permanent teeth will come through correctly, but it would be usual for them to.

Leaving Home

I like to home my puppies either at seven weeks of age or after ten weeks, as it is widely considered that puppies go through a 'fear period' between eight and ten weeks of age. Provided the new owner is happy to take the puppy at seven weeks, and I have managed to make my decisions about which ones I want to keep or not to keep, I think it is better for puppies to go through this period in their new homes and not to be moved during it. By now they should be happy, independent little characters who are ready for new horizons. It is also said that the optimum time for learning is between eight and twelve weeks of age, and most new puppies have a lot to learn in their new environments.

It is important that the puppy takes with him to his new home a diet sheet, complete with details of wormings including the names of products used. I usually give new owners a starter pack of food, so that they can see at first hand how easy it is to use and so that the puppy is guaranteed to start his new life on a diet that he is used to.

Hopefully, by the time the puppy is ready to go his registration papers will be back from the Kennel Club. The transfer of ownership with the English Kennel Club automatically gives the new owner of the puppy six weeks' free insurance cover and if for any reason, the papers are not back then I give new owners an alternative six weeks' cover with a pet insurance company. I have a pedigree written out ready for the new owner, which I sign, stating that it is correct to the best of my knowledge. I like to give new owners a copy of the Kennel Club Code of Ethics, which gives them a good idea of what is expected in responsible dog ownership. Lastly, I always instil into new owners the fact that if for any reason, at any time, they cannot keep the dog any longer, they should contact me immediately.

11
Ailments and Diseases

On the whole, English Springers are healthy dogs who should live a long and trouble-free life but, as with any breed, there are some inherent problems that can crop up occasionally, and other general ailments which you may encounter in the course of your Springer's life.

For his good health day-to-day management is necessary as outlined previously. His teeth and ears should be kept clean, his coat groomed regularly and any hair that is in danger of matting either kept combed through or cut off.

Vaccinations

By eight weeks of age, the natural immunity that the dog will have acquired from his dam will be weakening, and the first visit your puppy makes after coming home should be to your veterinary surgeon so that he can have his vaccinations. The requirements vary from country to country, but this need not worry you as your vet will know exactly what is needed and will be only too happy to explain to you what protection your puppy needs.

The English Kennel Club recommends that all breeding stock are tested under the joint Kennel Club/British Veterinary Association schemes for Hip Dysplasia, Progressive Retinal Atrophy (PRA) and Retinal Dysplasia (RD).

Hip Dysplasia

The inherited component of canine hip dysplasia is caused by the interaction of many genes, and the expression of these genes may be modified by environmental factors such as nutrition, trauma and exercise. Hence, it is possible for a puppy from two parents with good hip scores to have poor hips if due care and sensible management have not been provided when rearing the puppy. It is possible to have your dog's hips X-rayed after twelve months of age by your vet, who will (for a set fee) submit these X-rays to the British Veterinary Association for scoring. From the results of this test, you will be advised whether your dog is suitable to be bred from. What is considered a suitable score to breed on from varies from breed to breed, just as the level of importance placed on hip X-raying varies from country to country.

If you are at all concerned about your puppy's/dog's hips, the best thing to do is contact your vet. This is not a common problem in the UK but it is one that we should be aware of, particularly when rearing a puppy.

Progressive Retinal Atrophy

Progressive retinal atrophy (PRA) affects several breeds, and the English Springer is one of them. They can be affected by generalized PRA, which will eventually cause total blindness, or central PRA, which will cause either partial or total blindness. Dogs that are being bred from are normally tested annually, but this is not a totally successful method of control as PRA may not show itself until a dog is quite old. Also, it seems that the gene affecting PRA must be recessive as it is capable of skipping many generations. Although it is not a common problem in our breed, it is one that we are aware of.

Retinal Dysplasia

Retinal dysplasia in its simplest form is seen as a multiple folding of the retina, while the most severe type is non-attachment of the retina to the underlying choroid. The effect on sight varies from no apparent effect to total blindness.

Testing sessions for PRA and Retinal dysplasia are held by various canine societies all over the UK, and the results are printed on the registration papers of any progeny registered with the Kennel Club from tested parents (*see* Appendix).

Canine Fucosidosis

In the early 1980s we in the UK received news from Australia of this inherent disease, which had been found to be affecting English Springers in Australia. It was found that the disease also affected people, and a Mr Bryan Winchester of the Institute of Child Health in England was researching this problem. Mr Winchester agreed to blood-test English Springers in the UK in the hope that the results would help with his research. We had no knowledge of any cases in the UK but I agreed to have all of the dogs in my kennels blood-tested for signs of the disease. We found that almost half of my stock were carriers of fucosidosis. Further testing of kennels around the country showed that the disease was quite widespread and, although very few dogs were found that actually had the disease, many were carriers. The disease is easily diagnosed and, as a result of the responsible attitude taken by breeders, has been brought under control.

The following is a report on the disease by Mr W.R. Kelly of the Department of Veterinary Pathology and Public Health at the University of Queensland, Australia.

> Pathologists at the veterinary schools in Queensland and New South Wales have recently become aware of a heritable nervous disease known as fucosidosis, which appears to be established in several lines of English Springer Spaniel in Australia, and which is almost certainly present in the breed in the UK and USA.
>
> The disease shows up as an unexplained loss of weight, beginning at twelve months of age (perhaps earlier or later in some individuals), this is followed in a few months by steadily-worsening wobbliness of gait, change of voice, odd muscle spasms around the head and elsewhere and increasing difficulty in eating. There is no known cure for the disease and animals of both sexes can develop it.
>
> It has recently been shown that affected animals are totally deficient in a certain enzyme or chemical which is essential for the breakdown of a sugar (fucose) in body cells. This sugary substance therefore accumulates with time in many parts of the body, particularly in the brain and some nerves where the cells are longer-lived.
>
> The reason for the lack of the enzyme is that the individual is conceived without the gene which produces the enzyme. In order for a dog to have enough enzyme to have a normal life span it must have received at least one of these genes from either parent. Most dogs get two. With only one gene, a dog or bitch will have only half the normal amount of enzyme, this will however be enough for it to break down

the sugar and lead a normal life. Every pup from such an animal will have a 50 per cent chance of not getting this particular gene from this parent, and if the pup also misses out on this gene from the other parent, then the pup will develop fucosidosis later in life. The parents in this case, with only one gene each for the enzyme (fucosidase) are thus 'carriers' for this disease.

An important recent discovery was the finding that carrier Springers could be identified by chemical analysis of a blood sample, which in these animals can be shown to have only half the normal amount of the enzyme fucosidase. This of course means that breeders wishing to ensure that their breeding stock are not carriers will be able to do so.

Entropion

This is primarily an inherited condition which affects several breeds, some much worse than others. It is occasionally seen in English Springers, but fortunately it is not usually very severe. It is caused by an excess of eyelid tissue, or a small eye, or both, the result being that a varying amount of hair-covered eyelid can turn in to rub directly against the cornea, or conjunctiva, or both. As the hair rubs against the eye, so it makes the eye sore. In some dogs the signs of the problem are excessive blinking and a wet face caused by the eyes' running. In the less severe cases the hairs of the lower lid at the outer extremity are the only ones to rub on the eye, and sometimes, in these cases, the condition will correct itself as the puppy grows. In severe cases surgery will be necessary to rectify the problem. If at all concerned, contact your vet, who will probably give you some ointment to lubricate the eye of a still-growing dog while he monitors the situation.

Cataracts

The English Springer Spaniel is not one of the breeds listed as suffering from hereditary cataracts, although, of course, cataracts that develop as a result of PRA are caused by an inherent problem. Some cataracts are acquired as the result of trauma, uveitis, or diseases such as diabetes. Cataracts can vary in size, with the larger ones affecting vision and sometimes causing blindness. They are easy to see as a smoky discoloration on the eye.

Fits

This is a complex subject, and there are many different types and causes. The fit is a seizure, which in turn is a short-lived episode of abnormal motor or behavioural activity. The term epilepsy is often used to describe a fit or seizure. This term actually refers to any condition in which seizures are recurrent. The most familiar type of seizure is the one in which there is a brief loss of consciousness and convulsive muscle activity, often accompanied by salivation and involuntary defecation and urination. It is known that epilepsy is inherent in several breeds of dog, including the Welsh Springer Spaniel, and although it has not been proved to be inherent in the English Springer, we do occasionally hear of cases of dogs in the breed having fits.

Labial Eczema

This is an unpleasant condition that causes the dog some irritation and gives off an unpleasant odour. It occurs in the loose folds of skin on the lower lips and there does not seem to be any logical reason why it should affect some dogs and not others. It can be treated by bathing the affected area with a solution made up with either boiled water and TCP or boiled water and hydrogen peroxide. I have found the former helps to eliminate the unpleasant odour, but the latter is more effective at drying up the problem. If it is very severe then veterinary advice should be sought, and it may be considered necessary to operate to remove some of the loose skin.

Interdigital Cysts

These can sometimes be mistaken for a grass-seed reaction and take the form of a swelling between the toes. They will sometimes be eased by bathing in salt water, but if this does not help then it may be necessary for your vet to lance them.

Anal Glands

These small glands, situated on either side of the anus, do not

214

normally cause any problems. They contain a foul-smelling liquid which gets excreted naturally when faeces are passed or when the dog has a bad fright. They do, however, occasionally get blocked and cause the dog considerable discomfort. Should this happen, a trip to the vet's will be necessary to have them emptied. Your vet may advise you on a different diet for your dog to ensure that the faeces are sufficiently solid to assist in the natural action of emptying the glands. In severe, chronic cases, surgery is sometimes performed to remove the glands.

Diarrhoea and Sickness

These may happen simultaneously or separately, and are often nothing to worry about, having been caused by the dog eating something that has disagreed with him. Twenty-four hours' fasting will often cure the problem, followed on the next day with a bland diet of rice and chicken. If you do not wish to fast your dog, then dosing him with Arsen Alb 30, at a rate of one tablet every fifteen minutes for four tablets, and then one tablet three times a day should do the trick. Plenty of fresh water should be available to prevent dehydration. However, if your dog seems ill with the condition then do not hesitate to contact your vet.

Kennel Cough

This is caused by a virus which can be picked up almost anywhere, and does not generally cause any problems with the healthy adult dog. It may cause you a little concern at first, as the cough tends to sound rather as though the dog has something stuck in his throat, rather than a true cough. Vaccinations are available to guard against kennel cough and may be advisable before putting your dog into a boarding kennels.

Aural Resection

This is sometimes necessary if thickening of the integument occurs and, as a result, the ear canal gets smaller in diameter. This can cause the dog great discomfort and surgery can be the only answer.

It may possibly be put off or avoided by scrupulous care of the ear, but this is not always the case.

Coprophagia

Coprophagia, or eating faeces is a particularly revolting habit which may indicate a dietary deficiency. You can consult your vet or pet food manufacturer on the subject or try dosing the dog, or dogs, with Milk of Magnesia.

Mammary Tumours

These may occur in the older bitch, but less often in a bitch who has been spayed. They appear as hard lumps in the mammary glands of the bitch and their growth should be monitored and veterinary advice taken, as it may be considered necessary to remove them surgically.

Pyometra

This is a dangerous condition as, if it is allowed to develop, it can cause death. The early signs are that the bitch will be drinking more than is usual and will have a discharge from her vulva that is often smelly. She will appear off-colour and restless. This usually happens six to eight weeks after a season, and can sometimes occur in bitches who are in whelp, although this is not common. The condition will occasionally respond to treatment if caught early enough, but often it is necessary to remove the uterus surgically.

Parasites

These can be a problem, particularly in the summer months, with fleas, lice, mites and ticks all inclined to attack dogs. There are many excellent products now on the market to deal with these parasites, and to be sure of using the most up to date, I would advise taking veterinary advice, particularly if dealing with puppies, or in-whelp or nursing bitches.

Similarly, worms in the dog are a problem that are best dealt with on veterinary advice, and if a regular worming programme is set up on the advice of your vet, then there is no reason why they should present a problem to you or your dog.

Homeopathic Remedies

Where possible, I prefer to treat my dogs using homeopathic remedies. These are considered by many people to be safer, and less likely to cause side-effects, than conventional medicines. Before administering a homeopathic remedy to your dog, it is important to check the dosage recommended on the packaging and, if in doubt, to consult a homeopathic vet or ask for advice from the manufacturer.

Heatstroke

Heatstroke can very quickly be fatal, and should be treated as a real emergency. It is far more common than many people think, and often occurs as a result of a dog being left in a car on a hot day. It takes a very short time for the inside of a car to get very hot – even if the windows are left open a little – and dogs should never be left locked in cars on a summer's day (even if it is cloudy the cloud may clear while you are away and your dog could very quickly die).

Any animal that is suffering from heatstroke should be cooled immediately. The most effective way to do this is with cold water: the dog should be submerged in cold water if that is practical, otherwise hosed down or doused with cold water, or covered in wet cold towels or blankets, or ice packs if available. Rescue Remedy will help with the shock: two drops into the mouth every ten to fifteen minutes. The rectal temperature should be checked every fifteen minutes to ensure that the body is not over-cooled, and when the temperature drops to 102°F (38.8°C), the dog can be dried off and left to rest somewhere cool with access to cold drinking water. His temperature should be checked every half an hour to ensure that it does not rise again. After this initial first aid, the dog should be taken to the vet.

Shock

Shock can be caused by many different things and the cause will obviously need to be treated in its own right. However, shock itself can be treated with gentle handling, by reassuring the dog with your voice and by keeping his temperature steady; try to keep him warm without allowing him to overheat. Rescue Remedy, Aconite and/or Arnica can all be useful to help with the effects of shock, depending on the cause. Rescue Remedy will help with most shock cases: one or two drops administered to the mouth or lips every ten to fifteen minutes. Aconite will help with shock from illness where fever is evident: one tablet on the tongue every fifteen minutes for four tablets, and then three times per day for two or three days. Arnica will help with shock from trauma such as a blow or an accident, administered as for Aconite.

Poisoning

There are many different things that may cause poisoning in your dog and as with most cases listed in this book the best person to turn to for help is your veterinary surgeon. As a first-aid measure to induce vomiting in a dog known to have ingested a toxic, but non-corrosive substance, a crystal of washing soda pushed to the back of the tongue is usually effective. However it should be remembered that it only takes up to four hours for a dogs stomach to empty and so there is little point in causing vomiting beyond this time. If you know that the dog has swallowed a corrosive substance (like paint-stripper or bleach), do not induce vomiting as the corrosive may, on its way back to the mouth, cause further damage to the oesophagus and possibly gain entry to the lungs. Instead, administer water or milk to dilute the substance in the stomach and then take the dog to the vet. If you do feel that it is appropriate to make your dog vomit before he is attended to by a vet it may be useful to save some of the vomitus for future analysis.

Should your dog be bitten by a poisonous snake, such as an adder or viper, treatment with antihistamines should help while you are taking your dog to the nearest vet.

Veterinary First-Aid Kit

Whilst it is impossible to predict, and prepare for, any eventuality, it is well worth putting together a veterinary first-aid kit. I would suggest you include the following items:

Lint, bandages and elastoplast   (much as you would keep in your own first-aid kit)

A muzzle   This may be useful if your dog is in a lot of pain and reluctant to have a would dressed

Antiseptic   For washing wounds, diluted with water as instructed on packaging (salt water can be used as an alternative, mixed one teaspoon to 1 pint (½ litre) of water)

Crystal of washing soda   To induce vomiting (*see* poisoning)

A thermometer   Since a dog's temperature is taken from the anus, the thermometer should be kept solely for use in veterinary first aid

Antiseptic cream

Calendula ointment

Veterinary wound powder

Aconite 6   For fever and shock

Apis Mel 6   For stings

Arnica 6   For trauma of any type: bruising, blows, bite wounds, muscle injuries, and all sorts of shock from injuries and that occurring after anaesthetic

Arsen Alb 6   For vomiting and diarrhoea

Carbo Veg 30   May well help with excessive flatulence

Caullophyllum 30   *See* whelping

Gelsemium 6   For settling a frustrated male (dog) when he is unable to have access to an in-season bitch

Hypericum 6   For treating the nerve endings, in the feet for example: pinched toes, injured claws, etc.

Nux Vom 6   For uncomplicated gastritis

Rescue Remedy   For all types of shock and trauma

Appendices

I   UK Breed Standard of 1934

Characteristics

The English Springer is the oldest of our Sporting Gundogs and the taproot from which all of our sporting land spaniels (Clumbers excepted) have been evolved. It was originally used for the purpose of finding and springing game for the net, falcon, or greyhound, but at the present time it is used entirely to find, flush, and retrieve game for the gun. The breed is of ancient and pure origin, and should be kept as such. The Springer's gait is strictly his own. His forelegs should swing straight forward from the shoulder throwing the feet well forward in an easy and free manner, not a paddle nor choppied terrier-like stride. His hocks should drive well under his body following in a line with his forelegs. At slow movement many Springers have a pacing stride typical of the breed.

General Appearance

The general appearance of the modern Springer is that of a symmetrical, compact, strong, upstanding, merry, and active dog, built for endurance and activity. He is the highest on the leg and raciest in build of all land spaniels.

Head and Skull

The skull should be of medium length and fairly broad and slightly rounded, rising from the foreface, making a brow or stop, divided by a fluting between the eyes gradually dying away along the forehead towards the occiput bone, which should not be peaked. The cheeks should be flat, that is not rounded or full. The foreface should be of proportionate length to the skull, fairly broad and deep without being coarse, well chiselled below the eyes, fairly deep and square in flew, but not exaggerated to such an extent as would interfere with comfort when retrieving. Nostrils well developed, underjaw strong and level mouth, that is neither over nor under-shot.

Eyes

The eyes should be neither too full nor too small but of medium size, not prominent nor sunken but well set in (not showing haw) of an alert, kind expression. A mouse-like eye without expression is objectionable, as also is a light eye. The colour should be dark hazel.

Ears

The ears should be lobular in shape, set close to the head, of good length and width, but not exaggerated. The correct set should be in a line with the eye.

Neck

The neck should be strong and muscular, of nice length and free from throatiness, well set in the shoulders, nicely arched and tapering towards the head – this giving great activity and speed. A ewe neck is objectionable.

Forequarters

The forelegs should be straight and nicely feathered, elbows set well to body and with proportionate substance to carry the body, strong flexible pasterns.

Body

The body should be strong and of proportionate length, neither too long nor too short, the chest deep and well developed with plenty of heart and lung room, well-sprung ribs, loins muscular and strong with slight arch and well coupled, thighs broad and muscular and well developed.

Hindquarters

The hindlegs should be well let down from hips to hocks. Stifles and hocks moderately bent, inclining neither inwards nor outwards. Coarseness of hocks objectionable.

Feet

Feet tight, compact, and well rounded with strong full pads.

Tail

The stern should be low and never carried above the level of the back, well feathered and with a lively action.

Coat

The coat should be close, straight, and weather resisting without being coarse.

Colour

Any recognized Land Spaniel colour is acceptable, but liver and white, black and white, or either of these colours with tan markings preferred.

Weight and Size

The approximate height should be 20in. The approximate weight should be 50lb.

II Pedigrees of Famous Dogs

<table>
<tr><td colspan="3" align="center">PEDIGREE</td></tr>
<tr><td colspan="2">NAME Sh.Ch. Bella Bee of Kennersleigh
SEX Bitch
BORN 20 August 1961</td><td>OWNER Mrs J.M. Taylor
BREEDER Mrs M. Keighley</td></tr>
<tr><td align="center">PARENTS</td><td align="center">GRANDPARENTS</td><td align="center">GREAT
GRANDPARENTS</td></tr>
<tr><td rowspan="4">SIRE Ch. Studley Major</td><td rowspan="2">SIRE Boxer of Bramhope</td><td>SIRE Peter's Benefactor</td></tr>
<tr><td>DAM Bramhope Suzette</td></tr>
<tr><td rowspan="2">DAM Bountiful of Beechfield</td><td>SIRE Sh.Ch. Grand Lodge</td></tr>
<tr><td>DAM Soubrette of Happeedaze</td></tr>
<tr><td rowspan="4">DAM Belize of Bramhope</td><td rowspan="2">SIRE Am. Ch. Melilotus Shooting Star</td><td>SIRE Am. Ch. Greenfair's Game Lad</td></tr>
<tr><td>DAM Am. Ch. Melilotus Love Song</td></tr>
<tr><td rowspan="2">DAM Blackantan of Bramhope</td><td>SIRE Blackbuster of Bramhope</td></tr>
<tr><td>DAM Barnadine of Bramhope</td></tr>
</table>

PEDIGREE		
NAME Sh.Ch. Esholt Beujolais **SEX** Dog		**BORN** 8 October 1979 **OWNER/BREEDER** Mrs J. Hill
PARENTS	**GRANDPARENTS**	**GREAT GRANDPARENTS**
SIRE Sh.Ch. Malcou Dusty Miller	**SIRE** Ch. Pericles of Truelindale	**SIRE** Ch. Teesview Titus
		DAM Morag of Truelindale
	DAM Majeba Melody Maker	**SIRE** Sh.Ch. Hawkhill Connaught
		DAM Majeba Meg
DAM Barlochan Ebony Lace	**SIRE** Sh.Ch. Cleavehill Yankee Clipper	**SIRE** Ch. Teesview Tarmac
		DAM Cleavehill Mary Poppins
	DAM Sh.Ch. Barlochan Bellringer	**SIRE** Sh.Ch. Hawkhill Connaught
		DAM Cleavehill Sheba

PEDIGREE		
NAME Sh.Ch. Teesview Pandora of Truelindale **SEX** Bitch		**BORN** 2 January 1970 **OWNER** Mrs E. Dobson **BREEDER** Miss M. Alder
PARENTS	**GRANDPARENTS**	**GREAT GRANDPARENTS**
SIRE Ch. Teesview Titus	**SIRE** Am. Ch. Stokeley Toreador	**SIRE** Colmaris Son of George
		DAM Sh.Ch. Stokeley Sea Princess
	DAM Ch. Tyneview Margaret	**SIRE** Sh.Ch. Studley Brave Buccaneer
		DAM Tyneview Sarina
DAM Morag of Truelindale	**SIRE** Sh.Ch. Douglas of Freetwood	**SIRE** Ch. Alexander of Stubham
		DAM Glencora Tonga
	DAM Sh.Ch. Lessudden Linnet	**SIRE** Conniel Cavalier
		DAM Conniel Country Girl of Lessudden

PEDIGREE		
NAME Ch. Alexander of Stubham **SEX** Dog	**BORN** 20 February 1950 **OWNER/BREEDER** Mrs F.O. Till	

PARENTS	GRANDPARENTS	GREAT GRANDPARENTS
SIRE Boxer of Bramhope	**SIRE** Peter's Benefactor	**SIRE** Ch. Pleasant Peter
		DAM Pasture Toddy
	DAM Bramhope Suzette	**SIRE** F.T.Ch. Tim of Chastleton
		DAM Lilac Beauty
DAM Susan of Stubham	**SIRE** Chief of Staff	**SIRE** Hercules of Rafehill
		DAM Glenbrook Lass
	DAM Globeland's Roxa	**SIRE** Whadden Chase Robin
		DAM Belle of Globe

PEDIGREE		
NAME Sh.Ch. Hawkhill Connaught **SEX** Dog	**BORN** 11 July 1969 **OWNER/BREEDER** Mrs J. Hancock & Mr Cudworth	

PARENTS	GRANDPARENTS	GREAT GRANDPARENTS
SIRE Ch. Moorcliff Dougal of Truelindale	**SIRE** Sh.Ch. Douglas of Freetwood	**SIRE** Ch. Alexander of Stubham
		DAM Glencora Tonga
	DAM Sh.Ch. Lesudden Linnet	**SIRE** Conniel Cavalier
		DAM Conniel Country Girl of Stubham
DAM Sh.Ch. Slayleigh Paulina	**SIRE** Sh.Ch. Whadden Chase Drake	**SIRE** Ch. Alexander of Stubham
		DAM Whadden Chase Destiny
	DAM Quacker Girl of Stubham	**SIRE** Ch. Hyperion of Stubham
		DAM Brandyhole Fleur De Lys of Stubham

225

PEDIGREE		
NAME Sh.Ch. Wenark Justin Step **SEX** Dog **BORN** 5 May 1982		**OWNER** Grant & Clark **BREEDER** Mrs W. Clark
PARENTS	**GRANDPARENTS**	**GREAT GRANDPARENTS**
SIRE Sandale Song n Dance	**SIRE** Lyndora Lord of the Dance	**SIRE** Sh.Ch. Hawkhill Connaught
		DAM Lyndora April Dancer
	DAM Sh.Ch. Sandale Step Me Gaily	**SIRE** Sh.Ch. Hawkhill Connaught
		DAM Fenway Dreamtime at Sandale
DAM Wenark Cornflake	**SIRE** Diggle Jackadandy	**SIRE** Proud Knight of Diggle
		DAM Hawkhill Jasmine
	DAM Merrivew Sweet Harmony of Wenark	**SIRE** Feorlig Freemason
		DAM Koriston Deb's Delight

PEDIGREE		
NAME Sh.Ch. Grand Lodge **SEX** Dog **BORN** 14 April 1947		**OWNER** Mr R. Cleland **BREEDER** Miss E. Gault
PARENTS	**GRANDPARENTS**	**GREAT GRANDPARENTS**
SIRE Boxer of Bramhope	**SIRE** Peter's Benefactor	**SIRE** Ch. Pleasant Peter
		DAM Pasture Toddy
	DAM Bramhope Suzette	**SIRE** F.T.Ch. Tim of Chastleton
		DAM Lilac Beauty
DAM Jordanstown Lass	**SIRE** Ir. Ch. Templecorran Spotback	**SIRE** Mockerkin Domino
		DAM Templecorran Saddle Back
	DAM Glenmount Lass	**SIRE** Orpheus of Canfordborne
		DAM Carromoney Hill Degiuty

Ch. Mompesson Remember Me
Liver/white tricolour bitch

Owner: Mrs F. Jackson

Born: 13.11.86

Sh.Ch. Hawkhill Starsky
- Hawkhill Blakeney
  - Sh.Ch. Cavalier of Loweview
    - Ch. Douglas of Freetwood
    - Judy of Loweview
  - Hawkhill Milly Moss
    - Sh.Ch. Hawkhill Connaught
    - Sh.Ch. Hawkhill Hello Dolly
- Hawkhill Finians Rainbow
  - Sh.Ch. Hawkhill Finlandia
    - Fin. Ch. Mompesson Fisherman
    - Sh.Ch. Hawkhill Hello Dolly
  - Teesview Telma
    - Sh.Ch. Hawkhill Connaught
    - Teesview Talk of the Town

Mompesson Country Girl
- Sh.Ch. Raenstor Country Boy of Mompesson
  - Sh.Ch. Ackiltie Morton at Sandale
    - Hawkhill Blakeney
    - Lyndora Folk Dancer
  - Mompesson Charlies Angel
    - Sh.Ch. Hawkhill Crepello
    - Sh.Ch. Mompesson Wonderful Dream
- Mompesson Lucky Girl
  - Sh.Ch. Barlochan Engineer
    - Sh.Ch. Cleavehill Yankee Clipper
    - Sh.Ch. Barlochan Bellringer
  - Mompesson Lucky Dream
    - Sh.Ch. Hawkhill Starsky
    - Raenstor Lucky Charm

Ch. Chinoe's Adamant James
Liver/White Dog

Breeder: Ann H. Roberts
Owner: Dr Milton Prickett

Born: 1968

- **Ch. Salilyn's Aristocrat**
  - Ch. Inchidony Prince Charming
    - Ch. Salilyn's Citation II
      - Ch. Salilyn's Sensation, C.D.
      - Salilyn's Princess Meg
    - Ch. Salilyn's Cinderella II
      - Ch. King Peter of Salilyn
      - Ch. Walpride's Gay Beauty
  - Ch. Salilyn's Lily of the Valley
    - Salilyn's Royal Consort
      - Ch. Salilyn's Citation II
      - Ch. Ascot's Estralita
    - Salilyn's Glenda
      - Ch. King William of Salilyn
      - Ch. Salilyn's Good Omen
- **Ch. Canarch Inchidony Brook**
  - Ch. Inchidony Prince Charming
    - Ch. Salilyn's Citation II
      - Ch. Salilyn's Sensation, C.D.
      - Salilyn's Princess Meg
    - Ch. Salilyn's Cinderella II
      - Ch. King Peter of Salilyn
      - Ch. Walpride's Gay Beauty
  - Ch. Canarch Sunnyside, C.D.
    - Ch. Syringa Disc Jockey
      - Ch. Kaintuck Marc Anthony
      - Ch. Syringa Sue
    - Melilotus Hufty Tufty
      - Ch. Rostherne Hunter
      - Melilotus Princess Dona

228

Ch. Canarch Phantom
Liver and White

AKC No. 755148

Breeders: Charles and Mary Lee Hendee

Ch. Canarch Phantom

- **Can.Ch. Canarch Commandant**
  - **Ch. Brendon's Royal Command**
    - Ch. Telltale Royal Stuart
      - Ch. Telltale Author
      - Ch. Stepney's Cinderella
    - Ch. Palmlane's Tina Maginna
      - Ch. Telltale Author
      - Ch. Maginna's Royal Heiress
  - **Ch. Canarch Scored For Strings**
    - Ch. Chuzzlewit's Editorial
      - Ch. Winacko's Editor's Choice, C.D.
      - Canarch Contemplation
    - Ch. Canarch Soft Music
      - A.C.Ch. Canarch Inchidony Sparkler
      - Canarch Pastoral, T.D.
- **Ch. Canarch Mocha Charlotte, C.D.**
  - **Ch. Telltale Royal Stuart**
    - Ch. Telltale Author
      - Ch. Salilyn's Aristocrat
      - Telltale Victoria
    - Ch. Stepney's Cinderella
      - Ch. Salilyn's Private Stock
      - Ch. Salilyn's Delight
  - **Ch. Canarch Favorite Melody**
    - Ch. Bordalyn's By Request, C.D.
      - Ch. Canarch Cardinal's Lancer
      - Ch. Bordalyn's Begin Again, C.D.
    - Ch. Canarch Soft Music
      - A.C.Ch. Canarch Inchidony Sparkler
      - Canarch Pastoral, T.D.

Ch. Canarch Soft Music
Black and White

Breeders: Charles and Mary Lee Hendee

- A.C.Ch. Canarch Inchidony Sparkler
  - Ch. Inchidony Prince Charming
    - A.C.Ch. Salilyn's Citation II
      - Ch. Salilyn's Sensation, C.D.
      - Salilyn's Princess Meg
    - Ch. Salilyn's Cinderella II
      - Ch. King Peter of Salilyn
      - A.C.Ch. Walpride Gay Beauty
  - Ch. Canarch Sunnyside, C.D.
    - Ch. Syringa Disc Jockey
      - Ch. Kaintuck Marc Anthony
      - Ch. Syringa Sue
    - Melilotus Hufty Tufty
      - Ch. Rostherne Hunter
      - Melilotus Princess Dona
- Canarch Pastoral, T.D.
  - Ch. Salilyn's Classic
    - Ch. Salilyn's Encore
      - Ch. Salilyn's Colonel's Overlord
      - Ch. Salilyn's Something Special
    - Salilyn's Arista
      - Ch. Salilyn's Aristocrat
      - Ch. Valdarae's Pembroke Sea Mist
  - Oran Park Becky
    - Ch. Marjon's Black Is Beautiful
      - Ch. Canarch Inchidony Herald
      - Ch. Melilotus Beauty
    - Canarch Snappy Comeback
      - A.C.Ch. Canarch Kentucky Jigger
      - Canarch Magnetism

230

Sh.Ch. and Am.Ch. Rufton Recorder
Liver and White

Owner: Robert Cornthwaite   Born: 11.5.26

Boss of Glasnevin

- F.T.Ch. Rex of Avendale
  - Rivington Samson
    - F.T.Ch. Rivington Sam
    - Cellbridge Cross
  - Reva of Avendale
    - Denne Jester
    - Horsford Hyssop
- Vandoreen
  - Beechgrove Mark 'Em
    - F.T.Ch. Denne Duke
    - Beechgrove Nelly
  - Vandala
    - Beechgrove Filbert
    - Lively Vanda

Rufton Flirt

- Chum of Chancefield
  - Chancefield Jock
    - Foel Jack
    - Foel Dacia
  - Chancefield Cleo
    - F.T.Ch. Rivington Sam
    - Susie of the Cairnes
- Firecrest
  - Cornwallis Cavalier
    - Spot
    - Beannie
  - Fireworks
    - F.T.Ch. Rex of Avendale
    - Nell

Ch. Salilyn's Condor
Liver and White

Breeder: Salilyn Kennels
Owner: Julia Gasow

Born: 5.10.87

- **Ch. Salilyn's Dynasty**
  - Ch. Telltale Author
    - Ch. Salilyn's Aristocrat
      - Ch. Inchidony Prince Charming
      - Ch. Salilyn's Lily of the Valley
    - Telltale Victoria
      - Ch. Salilyn's Classic
      - Canarch Triple Crown
  - Ch. Stepney's Cinderella
    - Ch. Salilyn's Private Stock
      - Ch. Filicia's Bequest
      - Ch. Salilyn's Sonnet
    - Ch. Salilyn's Delight
      - Ch. Salilyn's Exclusive
      - Ch. Salilyn's Limited Edition
- **Ch. Salilyn's Emblem**
  - Ch. Salilyn's Private Stock
    - Ch. Filicia's Bequest
      - Ch. Salilyn's Classic
      - Ch. Kaintuck Pixie C.D.
    - Ch. Salilyn's Sonnet
      - Ch. Salilyn's Aristocrat
      - Salilyn's Pirate Queen
  - Ch. Salilyn's Prima Donna
    - Ch. Salilyn's Design
      - Ch. Salilyn's Classic
      - Ch. Salilyn's Applause
    - Ch. Salilyn's Preference
      - Ch. Salilyn's Exclusive
      - Ch. Salilyn's Something Royal

232

III   Crufts Winners since 1903

1903 No CCs, over 50lb 1st Chishill Will
25–50lb D: 1st Compton Frisk
25–50lb B: 1st Ch. Fansome
1904 No classes
1905 No CCs, Best dog Ark
Best bitch Ch. Fansome
1906 Thorington Flush (CC for B.O.B.)
1907 D: Ark
B: Tissington Bounce
1908 No CCs, Best dog Ch. Beechgrove
Donaldson
Best bitch Tissington Bounce
1909 D: Achmore
B: Theakston Belle
1910 D: Ch. Beechgrove Donaldson
B: Ch. Tissington Frocks
1911 D: Ch. Tissington Fact
B: Ch. Tissington Frocks
1912 D: Ch. Beechgrove Donaldson
B: Ch. Tissington Frocks
1913 D: Ch. Beechgrove Donaldson
B: Sh.Ch. Bush
1914 D: Sh.Ch. Beechgrove Cecil
B: Flit
1915 No CCs, B.O.B.; Horford Humour
1916 No CCs, B.O.B.: Linley Bess
1917 No CCs, B.O.B. Beechgrove Lalia
1921 D: Ch. Horsford Hetman
B: Sh.Ch. Little Sunray
1922 D: Ch. Flint of Avendale
B: Wootton Bramblebush
1923 D: Ch. Horsford Harbour
B: Ch. Laverstoke Pattern
1924 D: Sh.Ch. Boghurst Rover
B: Ch. Inveresk Careful
1925 D: Bram of Duart Lodge
B: Laverstoke Pink'Un
1926 D: Ch. Standard
B: Boghurst Signoretta
1927 D: Ch. Standard
B: L'Ile Ladybird
1928 D: Ch. Nuthill Dignity
B: Countess Craigie
1929 D: Ch. Beauchief Buchanan
B: Ch. Inversk Carminetta
1930 D: Ch. L'Ile Fifeloon
B: Ch. Admiration of Solway
1931 D: Ch. Beauchief Benefactor
B: Ch. Knapp Ruby

1932 D: Ch. Winning Number of
Solway
B: Ch. Constance of Marmion
1933 D: Ch. Achi Evement
B: *Ch. Higham Teal
1934 D: Sh.Ch. Rex of Auckwear
B: *Sh.Ch. Worthen Suspense
1935 D: *Ch. Winning Number of
Solway
B: Fanshawe Fury
1936 D: *Ch. Nimble of Hamsey
B: Ch. Roundwood Lass
1937 D: Ch. Nimble of Hamsey
B: *Ch. Roundwood Lass
1938 D: *Tom Thumb
B: Ch. Roundwood Lass
1939 D: Ch. Beauchief Boreal
B: *Ch. Roundwood Lass
1948 D: *Ch. Stokeley Bonny Boy
B: Ch. Sprightly of Happeedaze
1950 D: *Ch. Sandylands Shandy
B: Ch. Jess of Montcrief
1951 D:*Ch. Carnfield Albvic Legioner
B: Ch. Birkdale Beggarmaid
1952 D: *Ch. Stokeley Gay Boy
B: Ch. Tillan Toddy
1953 D: *Ch. Alexander of Stubham
B: Ch. Dinah of Stubham
1955 D: Ch. Stokeley Lucky
B: *Ch. Highham Topsy
1956 D: *Ch. Inverruel Raider
B: Ch. Bathsheba of Bramhope
1957 D:*Dryburgh Thistle
B: Sh.Ch. Stokeley Sea Princess
1958 D: *Ch. Print of Ardrick
B: Ch. Northdown Donna
1959 D: Ch. Colmaris Chancellor
B: *Ch. Northdown Donna
1960 D: *Ch. Alexander of Stubham
B: Sh.Ch. Onyx of Stubham
1961 D: Ch. Sir Knight
B: *Sh.Ch. Glencora Country Maid
1962 D: Ch. Hyperion of Stubham
B: *Sh.Ch. O'Malley's Tango of
Glenbervie
1963 D: *Sh.Ch. Benefactor of
Roundfield
B: Ch. Tyneview Margaret

233

1964 D: *Sh.Ch. Pencloe Driftwood
B: Sh.Ch. Conneil Cover Girl
1965 D: Sh.Ch. Paidmyre Mallard
B: *Sh.Ch. Slayleigh Paulina
1966 D: *Sh.Ch. Moorcliff Freetwood
Gamecock
B: Sh.Ch. Slayleigh Paulina
1967 D: *Sh.Ch. Persimmon of Shipden
B: Cedilla of Mortondawn
1968 D: *Ch. Teesview Titus
B: Ch. Weavervales Moorcliff
Farewell
1969 D: *Sh.Ch. Hawkhill Royal Palace
(also reserve group)
B: Sh.Ch. Hawkhill Derby
Daydream
1970 D: Hawkhill Bracken
B: *Sh.Ch. Hawkhill Derby
Daydream
1971 D: *Ch. Inverruel Pacemaker
B: Sh.Ch. Hawkhill St Pauli Girl of
Moorcliff
1972 D: *Sh.Ch. Hawkhill Connaught
B: Sh.Ch. Cleavehill Corn Dolly
1973 D: Ch. Sotherton Skywarrior
B: *Sh.Ch. Teesview Pandora of
Truelindale
1974 D: *Sh.Ch. Hawkhill Connaught
(also group)
B: Sh.Ch. Hawkhill Humble Duty
1975 D: Star of the Moss
B: *Sh.Ch. Mompesson
Wonderful Dream (also reserve
group)
1976 D: Sh.Ch. Cleavehill Yankee
Clipper
B: *Sh.Ch. Teesview Pandora of
Truelindale
1977 D: Sh.Ch. Michael of Blacon
B: *Sh.Ch. Hildarry Roast
Chestnut
1978 D: Ch. Cliffhill Julius
B: *Sh.Ch. Barlochan Bellringer
1979 D: *Sh.Ch. Thornlea Cascade (also
reserve group)
B: Sh.Ch. Monclare Jennifer Eccles
1980 D: Sh.Ch. Thornlea Cascade
B: *Sh.Ch. Jancliff Lovelace

1981 D: Sh.Ch. Graftonbury Genghis
Khan
B: *Sh.Ch. Monclare Jennifer
Eccles
1982 D: *Sh.Ch. Graftonbury Genghis
Khan
B: Sh.Ch. Windydale Whimsicle
Ways of Calvdale
1983 D: Sh.Ch. Graftonbury Genghis
Khan
B: *Sh.Ch. Windydale Whimsicle
Ways of Calvdale
1984 D: *Freeway Indian Summer
B: Sh.Ch. Lyndora Easy Come
Easy Go of Romaline
1985 D: *Sh.Ch. Graftonbury Genghis
Khan (also group)
B: Sh.Ch. Lyndora Easy Come
Easy Go of Romaline
1986 D: *Ch. Risdene Devils
Advocate
B: Sh.Ch. Bomaris Coral Dancer
1987 D: *Sh.Ch. Feorlig Country Classic
(also reserve group)
B: Sh.Ch. Whitemoor Malteeser
1988 D: Ch. Bomaris Envoy to Shipden
B: Sh.Ch. Kennair Cheri Amour
1989 D: Sh.Ch.Feorlig Van Der Valk
B: *Sh.Ch. Roandew Gemima
Jones
1990 D: Sh.Ch. Lyndora April Fool
B: *Debanza I'm In Clover
1991 D: *Sh.Ch. Feorlig Life Line
B: Secrista Penny Royal
1992 D: *Sh.Ch. Owen Glynn of Robil
B: Sh.Ch. Jaraina Jacqui Tyn
1993 D: *Sh.Ch. Crooksbarn Four
Seasons of Teesview
B: Sh.Ch. Chetruda Lancashire
Rose of Melverly
1994 D: *Wenark Wizard of Oz at
Bluewinds
B: Wadeson Jessica Fletcher
1995 D: *Sh.Ch. Chaun Chablais at
Lyndora
B: Sh.Ch. Mompesson
Cher'Delight

*Denotes B.O.B.

234

Useful Addresses

International English Springer Spaniel Clubs

English Springer Spaniel Field Trial Association
Mrs Mari Anderson
295 12/47th Avenue South
Auburn 98001
Washington
USA

English Springer Spaniel Club of New South Wales
Mr and Mrs J. Peters
245 Quarry Road
Ryde 2112
New South Wales
Australia

English Springer Spaniel Club of Victoria
Mrs S. Rickards
'Wogan'
RMB 10 Outlook Road
Aisbourne 3437
Victoria
Australia

Icelandic English Springer Spaniel Club
Mr R. Halldorsson
Adalstraeti 4
PO Box 381
Iceland

Spaniel Club d'España
Apartado 70
Majadahonda
28 220 Madrid
Spain

English Springer Spaniel Club of France
Mr L. Gourdel
17 Rue Bleriot
22600 Loudeac
France

Springer Klubben
Mrs H. Berggren
Box 1355 Vida
810 22 Arsunda
Sweden

English Springer Spaniel Clubs and Societies in the UK

The English Springer Spaniel Club

Mr A. Emeney
39 Dennis Road
Wyken
Coventry
CV2 3HL

The English Springer Spaniel Club of Scotland

Mr K. Simpson
25 Mid Street
Kettlebridge
Fife
KY7 7QQ

The English Springer Spaniel Club of Wales

Mrs D. Bettinson
Tir-Adam-Uchaf Farmhouse
Heol Adam Gelligaer
Hengoed
Mid Glamorgan
CF8 8FU

Antrim and Down Springer Spaniel Club

Mr S.J. McConnell
17 Ballymather Road
Nutts Corner
Crumlin
Co. Antrim
BT29 4UL

The English Springer Spaniel Club of Southern Ireland

Mr M. White
Cleevaun
662 Howth Road
Raheny
Dublin 5
Eire

Other Useful Names and Addresses

The English Springer Spaniel Welfare

Mr S. Muckett
133 Bude Crescent
Stevenage
Herts
SG1 2QR

The Kennel Club

1–5 Clarges Street
Piccadilly
London
W1Y 8AB

The Irish Kennel Club Ltd

Fottrell House
Unit 36
Greenmount Office Park
Dublin 6

The American Kennel Club

51 Madison Avenue
New York, NY 10010

The Australian National Kennel Council
Royal Show Grounds
Ascot Vale
Victoria 3032

Federation Cynologique International (FCI)
Rue Leopold 11
14 B-6530 Thuin
Belgium

Bibliography

Biddis K.J., MRCVS, *Homoeopathy in Veterinary Practice*, The British Homoeopathic Association (1981).

Bloomfield, Betty, *Nursing and Rearing Newborn Puppies*, Able Publishing (1994).

Gasow, Julia (with Fitzgerald, Kellie and Roggenkamp, Edward K.), *The New Complete English Springer Spaniel*, Howell Book House Inc. (1994).

Hampton, Olga M.C., *All about the English Springer Spaniel*, Pelham Books (1980).

Moorland Hooper, Dorothy, *The Springer Spaniel*, Popular Dogs Publishing Co. Ltd (4th edn revised, 1975).
The Spaniel Owner's Encyclopedia, Pelham Good Companions' Library (1967).

Smith, Beatrice P., *The English Springer Spaniel in North America*, The English Springer Spaniel Field Trial Association Inc. (1970).

Turner, Trevor, BVet Med, MRCVS, FRSH, *Veterinary Notes for Dog Owners*, Popular Dogs Publishing Co. Ltd (1990).

Index